PRAISE

'In its beginning and at its end, *Toxic* is a meditation on home . . . [Flanagan] challenges us to open our eyes and face the truth of diminishment—not just of the natural world but of ourselves.' *Australian Book Review*

'Flanagan has produced noted works of journalism over the years but the truths he tells of the salmon industry are indeed stranger than fiction. While *Toxic* takes apart the Atlantic salmon industry scale-by-scale, it also offers hope.' *Tasmanian Times*

'Powerful . . . shed[s] light on the truth lurking below the surface.' *Sydney Morning Herald*

'Richard Flanagan is among the most versatile writers in the English language. That he is also an environmental activist and the author of numerous influential works of nonfiction makes his achievement all the more remarkable.' Joyce Carol Oates, *New York Review of Books*

TOXIC

The Rotting Underbelly of the
Tasmanian Salmon Industry

RICHARD FLANAGAN

PENGUIN BOOKS

PENGUIN BOOKS

UK | USA | Canada | Ireland | Australia
India | New Zealand | South Africa | China

Penguin Books is part of the Penguin Random House group of companies
whose addresses can be found at global.penguinrandomhouse.com

First published by Penguin Books in 2021

Cover photography by Shutterstock
Cover design by Adam Laszczuk © Penguin Random House Australia Pty Ltd
Author photograph by Joel Saget
Internal design by Post Pre-press, Australia
Typeset in 11.75/15.5 Maiola by Post Pre-press, Australia

Printed and bound in Australia by Griffin Press, part of Ovato, an accredited
ISO AS/NZS 14001 Environmental Management Systems printer

 A catalogue record for this
book is available from the
National Library of Australia

ISBN 978 1 76104 437 3

penguin.com.au

If we purchase the commodity,
we participate in the crime.

William Fox, 1791

For all the brave women who helped me write this book.

1

AT THE BEGINNING ITS SEA WAS RICH AND wondrous. We'd snorkel and fish and swim and beach-comb. Marvelling. So many people came to visit and stayed with us in that old vertical board shack on Bruny Island. And everyone felt it was one of those special, magical places.

The shack became our family's heart-place. Soon it also became where I went to write. I'd live there for up to six months of the year. It combined teeming life with an improbable serenity so pronounced it was possible to distinguish birds—an eastern rosella, say, from a shrike thrush—by the noise their wings made cutting the air. For near twenty-five years its beauty, its wonder, its lively tranquillity, fed my writing.

The large waterway on to which the shack faced, D'Entrecasteaux Channel, was famous for its scallops, its oysters and flathead. Crayfish and abalone could be had. I would boast to friends of how the place crawled with life. Penguins nested under our shack; I'd wake in the middle of the night to the soft sound of dolphins breaching, and increasingly whales were returning.

In 2002 I became aware of noise from a small salmon farm a kilometre and a half across the water, a farm so inconsequential I had never really thought about it. I reported the noise to the Tasmanian government department responsible, the Marine Farming Branch. They investigated, the noise stopped, and it seemed an end of things.

Then in 2005 noise returned.

This time everything was different. The farm had a new operator: Tassal, the largest salmon company in Tasmania. The company had a chequered past, and had only recently come out of receivership. Announcing a new focus on growing, and slashing costs, it had purchased Aquatas, the previous operators of the farm.[1] With others, I went back to the government.

A senior bureaucrat at the Marine Farming Branch was very clear: Tassal, he said, was a nightmare. I can't do anything, he said, leaning back in his chair and folding his hands behind his head. If I do something, Tassal rings the minister's office, and the minister's office rings me. So I can't help.

I have often thought about that strange day since. Government no longer seemed to be government, regulators no longer were burdened by the need to regulate, rule breakers had through an incomprehensible metamorphosis become rule makers, and the new rules seemed made not by parliament but by a profit-and-loss ledger—by, in other words, greed.

The senior bureaucrat advised us that our only hope was to deal directly with Tassal.

And for the next fifteen years we did.

Over fifteen years you might expect any industrial operation, particularly one with concerned neighbours, to gradually become quieter and cleaner. You would certainly expect government to improve regulation. But that's not what happened. The government regulators did nothing. As salmon farming industrialised, the farm grew larger, noisier and filthier, flogging our waters harder and harder, a Tassal senior employee once confiding that they breached their stocking limits there by 50 per cent.

For fifteen years our community tried to find an honourable compromise with Tassal. None of us wanted a fight. We wanted the beauty and happiness of our world to continue. That was all. We didn't like the growing evidence of marine pollution, of a struggling marine ecosystem, but we felt these were beyond our tiny influence, so we restricted our entreaties to noise only. We didn't like the salmon farm, but we felt compelled to accept it in a live and let live spirit.

But while we let Tassal live, things began to die.

The water, once so clear, grew turbid with the pollution from the farms—uneaten food pellets, the tonnes of fish shit that fell to the sea floor below the cages, a sludge slowly swept by tide and current through the greater waterway that is D'Entrecasteaux Channel. Algal growths fed by the massive nutrient outflows from the sludge began appearing on the rocks and on the seagrass beds. The seagrass began to retreat. Yet the process was slow, so slow as for a long time to be almost imperceptible.

Some things, though—strange things—were unmistakeable: there were fewer and fewer fish, there was more and more noise, and the farm began to take on the appearance of a heavy industrial site. Everything began accelerating. From being few fish to catch there were suddenly none. Great factory ships with their huge diesel engines now beat up and down the Channel 24/7. Sometimes they set up at the farm opposite and worked day and night, the noise, as one neighbour put it, like the sound of a semi-trailer reversing under your bedroom window.

Whenever the community complained, Tassal responded with evasions and little action. What little they would do, we would discover was soon undone. When pushed, they deceived and dissembled. Every promise Tassal made to our community, they finally broke. Every agreement Tassal made, they ultimately dishonoured. When pressed, Tassal would argue the farm was within regulations, though there were very few regulations, and what regulations existed were weak, and were, in any case, never enforced. There was no cop on the beat.

When it came to the salmon industry, we found ourselves with no rights as citizens. Like favela residents in Rio de Janeiro who, because the police won't enter favelas, have to ask drug lords to administer justice, we had no choice but to seek redress for the salmon farm's problems from the salmon farmers. And what we met was an industry so drunk on its own power that rather than address these many problems, it happily worsened them, opening up nearby zombie leases as new farms without notice or consultation, secure in the knowledge that locals were powerless, that no one dared stop the industry, and that the government and its bureaucrats would do nothing.

We were condemned to live amid the immense damage done when government abrogates its responsibilities and the only legislator is greed. And so, when we began noticing these changes, we tried to ignore them. Because we knew we were powerless. As well as noise, algae and slime kept increasing. And as they increased, other things mysteriously disappeared.

Fourteen years ago, I saw my last abalone. Eleven years ago, my last crayfish. Ten years ago, the penguins vanished. Then the cod. Then the tiny maireener shells disappeared—the same shells that Truganini and her people once gathered at the north end of Langford's Beach with which to make their necklaces. The water lost its clarity as more and more fish shit poured into the Channel. More algae. More of the coastline rimed with a bright-green slime. More of a strange bubbly brown broth on the once clear water's top.

And we tried to ignore these things; we tried to pretend they weren't happening.

I tried to ignore how, when I kayaked, the water felt different, dead rather than alive, sad rather than joyful, how it was now full of strange jellyfish blooms. I tried to pretend the waterway, once so serene, wasn't vibrating all the time from the salmon companies' giant factory ships thumping up and down daily, hourly. We didn't speak about how no one saw dolphins anymore. We didn't speak when the seahorses disappeared. When the weedy seadragons disappeared. When the striped cowfish were no more. When the seagrass started vanishing. We did talk two years ago about how the flathead were gone, but then we stopped, because it was too sad and everyone knew why they were gone.

And I felt so ashamed.

I'd had many friends come and stay because I was so proud of our island. But now I felt disgust and weariness, a shame too deep, until writing this, to be named. I stopped asking them. The noise would often be constant, twenty-four hours a day for weeks, and through summer sometimes months, on end.

Last year I had planned to spend six months at Bruny finishing a new novel. But the noise was intolerable. Worse, the sea seemed sick and I felt an unbearable sadness, and I had to leave. For the first time in almost a quarter of a century I didn't finish a novel at Bruny. After twenty-three years I had been driven from my workplace. I felt sick and cold and lost, as if something fundamental had been stolen from me and my home defiled by thieves as I lay sleeping.

Only now can I see that all that time, those many, many years, that long sleep, we were being played for fools by Tassal. We were tricked into colluding in the slow death of everything we loved, the destruction of everything that had enabled me to write my books. Because while we acted in good faith, Tassal was acting in bad faith.

They have destroyed what we loved. They have stolen our water, our serenity, and our beauty. They are killing our Channel, one of Tasmania's most beloved and iconic waterways, and, worse, its creatures. And unless checked, they will destroy so much more of what is unique and offers Tasmania a future in the twenty-first century.

The salmon farm opposite my shack has more than a million living fish packed into swirling vortexes of filth. The term 'farm' is a polite misnomer for what is in reality a floating feedlot. In just a little more than thirty years these floating feedlots have grown from one fish pen to huge cages scarring much of south-east Tasmania's once iconic coast, from the Tasmanian Peninsula to Bruny Island to the Huon Valley, as well as the west coast's Macquarie Harbour—and, worse, they are destroying much of these coastal areas' marine environment.

I began talking to others about what had happened. Each person would suggest someone else, and in this way I met professional fishermen, abalone divers, scientists, bureaucrats, academics, doctors, shackies, and local after local. I discovered that an industry parading as clean, green and healthy is in so many ways the exact opposite; that its claims of world's best practice and high environmental standards are no more than slick marketing to hide a legacy of environmental destruction, bullying, grossly inadequate regulation and questionable political influence, in service of producing a highly artificial but profitable protein. I learnt that the Tasmanian salmon industry—today valued at a billion dollars[2]—plans to double in size over the next decade.[3] I learnt that with its present practices, such a goal is only achievable by a further massive grab of public waters—likely to be announced in the first half of 2021—with the considerable and possibly irreparable environmental damage that will ensue.

And I discovered one community after another around southern Tasmania that had been similarly lied to and deceived as we had been, and worse, as we had also been, betrayed by our government and sold out by our regulators. I found that the salmon industry had few friends among ordinary Tasmanians. I met people whose lives had been broken by salmon farming, their soul worlds destroyed by a rogue industry. I met whistle-blowers in government and industry and science who had had enough; brave person after brave person prepared to go on the record. Their stories were shocking: a deeply disturbing web of intimidation, threats, public and corporate malfeasance, environmental destruction, and a food product the ingredient list of which would frighten the least food conscious.

I found myself falling deeper and deeper into the story of what happened, and how it happened, and all that is being destroyed to make the Tasmanian salmon we eat.

2

CHRISTINE COUGHANOWR IS A GENTLY spoken woman of large achievement. An estuarine scientist, she started and led for twenty years a remarkable program to clean up pollution and restore marine life in Hobart's magnificent Derwent Estuary. Known as the Derwent Estuary Program (DEP), it secured support from all levels of government and private industry to measure and improve the health of the Derwent's lower reaches. Over two decades, industry and councils, along with the state and federal governments, significantly reduced the pollution emptying into the Derwent. It was a successful and popular program that continues to enjoy considerable community support. But now Coughanowr fears that much that was achieved over the last two decades could be lost to the salmon corporations' greed.

Coughanowr is worried. She talks of Hobart's drinking water also now being at risk from the pollution from salmon hatcheries, where the salmon are bred and raised to smolt (juvenile) stage. The older hatcheries—which is most of them—disperse their nutrient-rich effluent straight back into the river from which they draw their freshwater. Many of these hatcheries are situated on the upper reaches of the Derwent and Huon river systems, both sources of drinking water, the Derwent providing the majority of Hobart's drinking water. Also present may be antibiotics and chemicals such as formaldehyde.

Another scientist, who spoke on the condition of anonymity, laments to me how rather than managing Hobart's drinking water for public risk, the Environment Protection Authority (EPA)—Tasmania's environmental regulator—gives the appearance of existing only to enable the expansion of the salmon industry. Rather than improving hatchery standards to an acceptable level, it sanctions more and larger hatcheries on Hobart's water catchment. Basic measures such as drum filters do not address the vast amount of dissolved nutrients—ammonia, nitrate, phosphorus—which hatchery fish release through their gills, along with decayed faeces and food, into the source of drinking water for half Tasmania's population.

Ammonia and nitrite are directly toxic to fish and invertebrate life in rivers and lakes. But that is not all, nor is it the greatest risk to the downstream environment.

Tasmanian rivers and lakes are nitrogen and phosphorus limited. Once these elements are introduced in quantity, algal growth can rapidly reach bloom proportions. If the nutrient load is high, pristine lakes and rivers can be quickly transformed from glorious clear waterways into turbid green algal-dominated environments.

Coughanowr explains that in 2015, following the opening by Huon Aquaculture of a large smolt hatchery below Meadowbank dam on the Derwent River, green algal blooms began appearing in the river. So extreme were these blooms that they threatened internationally significant seagrass beds and wetlands around Granton, an area sometimes described as the kidneys of the Derwent. At the same time, there was a public outcry about the bad taste and bad smell of Hobart's drinking water—water locals normally hail as the best-tasting in Australia. But now the water often stank and tasted awful. The bad taste and odour came from the blue-green algal blooms, which have occurred most summers since.

There is a strong likelihood that the algal blooms were caused by excess nitrogen flowing into Hobart's water catchment. Coughanowr says that TasWater's own research came to the same conclusion. The question, she says, is where does the nitrogen come from? There could be several sources, principally either agriculture or the cumulative effect of other sources. But the main agricultural sources lie on the Derwent *above* the Huon hatchery, where there have never been any significant algal blooms. All the algal blooms occur *below* Huon Aquaculture's new hatchery which has, according to Coughanowr, a nutrient discharge similar in size to a sewage plant of a town of 5–10,000 people.

To Coughanowr's astonishment there was no environmental impact statement for the hatchery, or if there was, she never saw it, as she would have expected to as director of the DEP. The EPA has never investigated whether the taste and odour compounds are produced or stimulated by the nutrients from the Meadowbank hatchery.

Coughanowr is frustrated at the lack of honest dialogue about the many issues associated with Big Salmon, and the ensuing loss of trust within the community. She talks of the good people she knows working within state bodies, salmon companies and research bodies as scientists, regulators and managers, who, she says, are hampered by commercial-in-confidence gags and by genuine risks to their long-term job prospects should they speak too directly.

TasWater, charged with managing Tasmania's drinking water and formed out of regional authorities in 2013, inherited an ill-considered agreement made in 2000 to supply farmers in the dry south-east of

Tasmania with Hobart's treated drinking water for them to use for irrigation. Improbable as this sounds, TasWater enlarged the commitment in 2014.

As an interim measure to deal with the taste and odour problems that began in 2015, TasWater installed an extra carbon filtration system at Bryn Estyn, its water treatment plant on the Derwent River. Costing $2.3 million since inception, the problem with the new filtration system has been that it takes longer to produce potable water. At the height of the summer of 2019–20, when farmers needed to use Hobart's drinking water for irrigation, the system couldn't produce it quickly enough. This, combined with below average rainfall, saw all Hobart put on to water restrictions and farmers similarly offered a reduced supply.

And so after deciding to spend millions of water users' money to address a problem that would appear to have been in no small part created by the salmon industry, Tasmanians had to endure a summer of water restrictions which had little to do with water supply and everything to do with water pollution. What begins with a refusal to confront the all-powerful salmon industry ends up a series of cascading crises that affect—and cost—Tasmanians.

The scandal of Hobart's water doesn't end there, though. In 2020 the EPA approved construction of Tassal's—and Australia's—largest hatchery yet, a few kilometres upstream of the Huon Aquaculture hatchery, compounding a crisis that in Tasmania cannot be named nor addressed and in the ensuing silence only worsens.

Bodies like TasWater, instead of choosing to manage its water catchments by asking hard questions of the salmon companies—as might be expected when dealing with the purity of the drinking water of its citizens and their very health—choose *not* to address the issues of water pollution that the algal blooms so clearly signalled. In reply to questions put to it in March 2021 about its management of nutrient pollution in Hobart's drinking water catchment, TasWater pleaded its 'limited ability . . . to implement catchment management activities in the Derwent catchment due to its size and scale'.

In what could be viewed as a political decision to avoid a fight with the all-powerful salmon industry, TasWater has now embarked on the largest water infrastructure project in its history, a $240 million upgrade of Bryn Estyn, fitting it with an advanced filtration system that will remove the bad taste and odours from the water.[4] Tasmania's water users will have to pay off a $240 million bill in part to deal with the consequences of Big Salmon's growing contamination of Tasmania's principal drinking water catchment, effectively subsidising the salmon corporations' profits and sanctioning their pollution.

The Tasmanian government and the salmon industry love to talk of the benefits salmon farming brings. But they don't talk about the many costs. When the contamination of Hobart's drinking water, water restrictions and hundreds of dollars of taxpayers' money being spent as a corrective are added up, Tasmanians might reasonably ask why they are paying hidden subsidies and what do they get out of the salmon industry in direct return.

The short answer is almost nothing.

If we look at what the Tasmanian government earns in lease and licence fees in exchange for the exploitation of and environmental damage to its iconic public waters from this billion-dollar industry, the amount is laughable. According to an Australia Institute analysis, the estimated total lease and licence fees of $923,008 represent about 0.1 per cent (one-thousandth) of the total farmgate production of the salmon industry in Tasmania, and 0.02 per cent of total state revenue.[5]

Coughanowr is now even more worried by the huge expansion of the salmon industry into Storm Bay on the east of Bruny Island at three massive lease sites. She hands me a graph in which the column showing the planned nutrient discharges—with 70 per cent of the nitrogen in fish feed excreted by salmon in the form of faeces and ammonia—from the Storm Bay floating feedlots dwarfs the column showing all sewage from Tasmania.

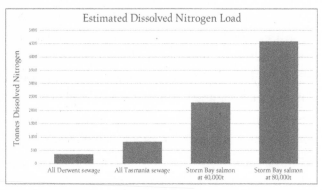

Source: Derwent Estuary Program Submission on Storm Bay Marine Farming Development Plan, 2018, p. 3

If the industry's plan of 80,000 tonnes of annual production is realised, it will be the equivalent of building a city of three million people (Brisbane, *plus* another 600,000) on North Bruny Island—and pouring all their sewage into Storm Bay.

This raises an even grimmer possibility than the contamination of Hobart's drinking water by the salmon industry.

In the 1970s, Hobart's Derwent Estuary was famously compared to Japan's globally notorious Minamata Bay. There, a factory poisoned the bay with mercury, which then poisoned and killed the local fish-eating people.[6] Minamata became a byword for industrial pollution and its murderous consequences. Because of unregulated pollution through much of the twentieth century from two principal factories, a zinc works and a pulp mill, the Derwent Estuary was poisoned to close to the same levels as Minamata Bay with heavy metals[7] and has, in consequence, some of the highest concentrations of mercury, zinc, lead, cadmium and arsenic in the world.[8] Over recent decades, much of the ongoing pollution has been cleaned up and the remnant heavy metals become sandwiched beneath cleaner sediment, effectively removing them from the marine ecosystem.

Then scientists' work revealed that when the sea's oxygen levels sank too low—a condition known as hypoxia—previously trapped heavy metals could be dragged back up and released into the marine ecosystem by biochemical processes.[9] Hypoxia can occur when algal blooms die off and sink to the sea floor where, in the process of rotting, they draw oxygen from the sea water. Algal blooms are, in turn, stimulated by excess nutrients.

For this reason, the key to managing the critical risk of heavy metal pollution in the Derwent Estuary was to minimise the possibility of algal blooms by reducing nutrient discharges. For the DEP, reducing nutrient pollution from sewerage systems became not just important of itself but also an urgent measure to stop the re-poisoning of the Derwent River Estuary and its marine life with heavy metal. To this crucial end hundreds of millions of taxpayers' and industry dollars were spent.

Coughanowr realised, however, that the scale of the salmon farmers' gigantic expansion into Storm Bay could reverse these millions of dollars of investment and decades of work cleaning up the Derwent by massively increasing nutrient levels in the previously pristine waters of the bay.

According to Coughanowr, if just 5 per cent of the nutrient discharge from the North Bruny expansion, located near the estuary mouth, entered the Derwent, it would effectively cancel out the most recent $50 million sewage treatment plant upgrade, which was specifically designed to reduce nutrients. She spearheaded a detailed submission from the DEP that highlighted this and other problems to the Marine Farming Planning Review Panel when in 2018 it was discussing approvals and conditions for the expansion into Storm Bay.

Yet when environmental scientist Louise Cherrie raised exactly this issue—of the massive effluent discharge and the possible remobilisation of heavy metals—as a member of the panel, she recalls only one panel member, Professor Colin Buxton, commenting, to dismiss such a potential risk.

A scientist with extensive experience working with resource and heavy industries, Louise Cherrie came on to the Marine Farming Planning Review Panel in

January 2018.[10] She believed in a sustainable salmon industry and felt she could help the industry as it came out of a crisis in the wake of a disastrous failed expansion at Macquarie Harbour. She found support in Professor Barbara Nowak, a specialist in aquatic animal health and biosecurity, who came on to the panel at the same time.

The panel was widely understood—including by Cherrie and Nowak—as being an independent Tasmanian government body charged with providing advice to the minister about whether fish farms should or should not be approved, and, if approved, under what conditions.

But this was not the case.

It was a convenient idea for the salmon industry and government, giving the appearance of proper process and probity. In 2011 the panel, for the only time in its history, had refused a plan by Tassal for the expansion of a fish farm in D'Entrecasteaux Channel over a unique, ecologically rich reef at a site called Soldiers Point. The expansion would have killed the reef, which was considered rare by University of Tasmania scientists. Another brave scientist, Dr Lois Koehnken, a highly respected water quality and river scientist, was then a panel member and was seen as central to that refusal.

'As a scientist you seek the truth, you tell people the risks,' was how Dr Koehnken explained the way she conducts her work to me. 'And you assume decisions will reflect this information.'

In the wake of the Soldiers Point refusal, that assumption could no longer be taken for granted. On 29 August 2011—four months after the decision— Dr Koehnken was replaced on the panel by Professor Colin Buxton.[11] Buxton had been publicly vocal in his advocacy of super-trawlers in Tasmanian waters[12] and in 2013 declared 'consumers should throw away their sustainability shopping guides, because all wild catch fish in Australia is sustainable'.[13] Groups such as the Tasmanian Conservation Trust did not regard Buxton as 'an appropriate person to provide balanced and independent scientific input to the panel's deci-sions . . . he has a very strong leaning towards the interest of fishing and aquaculture industries'.[14]

Within three months of Buxton's appointment, the three salmon companies applied to expand the salmon farming leases in Macquarie Harbour by 60 per cent— the largest expansion of salmon farming in Tasmania's history. A week later, in December 2011, the then Tasmanian Labor government, with Liberal support, introduced amending legislation, the effect of which was to ensure that the Marine Farming Review Panel never again rejected a salmon company plan: power to approve or reject a new fish farm now belonged with the minister. Defending the legislation in Parliament, the then minister, Bryan Green, 'explicitly stated that the amendments were proposed in response to that [Soldiers Point] decision'.

While there was a public outcry about possible environmental damage, the lack of baseline data, and potential impact on the endangered maugean skate, the minister made it clear in a letter later that month that the amending legislation's failure to address the *lack* of any rights of appeal against any decision made about salmon farming plans was 'intentional'.[15]

The public had been locked out.

With those changes the looming tragedy of Macquarie Harbour became inevitable—and in these dry details of governance it is possible to glimpse the chronicle of a death foretold. The panel became one more piece of the elaborate window dressing of a rogue industry that seemed to have the rules made up to suit its own bottom line. No new fish farm application could now be refused.

Seven years later, Louise Cherrie told me that she found 'little to no appetite for genuine discussion'. Her 'strong advice' to the panel was that their decision about Storm Bay be delayed for eighteen months to allow for proper scientific modelling to be done. To Cherrie it was very clear that the remobilisation of heavy metals was a plausible problem. Buxton asked, how does that even happen?

'Heavy metals in Derwent seafood are a known risk,' Cherrie explained to me. 'Metals bound up in sediment could be remobilised with high nutrient loads. Mercury is the big issue for seafood. It is in a reasonably non-bioavailable form, but remobilisation means it can accumulate up through the food web and into wild fish species. If consumed, it then has serious health effects. The environmental disaster in Minamata Bay in Japan that caused death and mutation of foetuses was from methylated [remobilised] mercury in seafood.'

The wild fishery was threatened. The recreational fishery was threatened. The lucrative abalone fishery was threatened. *Human beings were threatened.*

Like Coughanowr, like Koehnken, Barbara Nowak had come to Tasmania, fallen in love with its beauty, and stayed. She had worked closely with the Tasmanian salmon industry from its earliest days. Like Cherrie, a supporter of a sustainable salmon industry, Nowak was aware of the growing issues around the industry and went on to the panel believing that she could support the industry by contributing to responsible planning. But she was to discover that was not possible.

Professor Nowak was on the panel in no small part because of her expertise on biosecurity and yet there was no up-to-date biosecurity plan for Storm Bay—or, for that matter, any salmon farm in Tasmania. From a biosecurity point of view, Professor Nowak found that the proposed proximity of farms 'defied common sense'. She was told by other members that there was no point discussing or reviewing anything because in their view the minister would approve the expansion anyway.

Describing the panel sittings as 'soul destroying', Professor Nowak like Louise Cherrie had the strong sense that other members of the panel were regularly consulting with senior salmon company figures while making what was meant to be an independent, arms-length decision.

'Indeed,' the two women later wrote in their submission to the Legislative Council Inquiry, 'the salmon industry had ready access to the panel to advise . . . and were consulted on frequent basis and at a minute [sic] notice to the Panel'.[16] Cherrie, on the other hand, after doing 'due diligence', verifying information and data provided 'to determine whether operators had earned the right to grow', discovered 'extremely concerning information and the only reasonable view I could form was that Storm Bay developments should not proceed as proposed'. Yet when she tried to present this new information to the panel she was told it was 'too late to raise issues'.[17]

'It became very apparent that the panel did not consider other stakeholders,' Professor Nowak says.

She was told, 'We can't stop the Storm Bay development.' When Nowak and Cherrie pushed back, arguing that they should learn from the catastrophe of Macquarie Harbour, they were told Macquarie Harbour was irrelevant to the Storm Bay proposal.[18]

By tonnage of production, what was being proposed was Tasmania's biggest ever industrial development. And yet there was no foundation for such a development—no adequate science to explain what would happen to these massive nutrient loads; there was an inadequate biosecurity plan, no biogeochemical model and no regulatory standard to hold the corporations to account. Both Cherrie and Nowak were profoundly concerned that Storm Bay was at risk of going the same way as Macquarie Harbour. Yet one of the worst man-made ecological catastrophes in Tasmania in the last twenty years was a cataclysm the panel had 'an unwillingness to discuss and learn from'. [19]

Macquarie Harbour is a large inland harbour, six times the size of Sydney's, located in Tasmania's southwest, a third of which lies in the Tasmanian World Heritage Area. For scientists it is a fascinating inland waterway. For the salmon companies it looked a potential bonanza. A small salmon farm had been there since the 1980s, and the salmon farmers knew that the harbour's globally unique marine ecology meant it was free from the disease that ravaged its farms elsewhere in Tasmania and cost them so much money. They saw the giant harbour as perfect for growth with cheap production costs.

Others disagreed. Local salmon farmer Ron Morrison, as well as environmentalists and scientists, warned that the unique nature of the shallow harbour meant any large growth in salmon farming would inevitably result in an environmental catastrophe. They were ignored.

In 2012, Tassal and Huon Aquaculture began a gigantic expansion in Macquarie Harbour, which within six years triggered the very disaster that had been predicted. But instead of acting, the EPA and Tassal turned a crisis into a tragedy, doubling down on further expansion, and in Tassal's case overstocking farms already breaching pollution thresholds.

By 2015, monitoring revealed dorvilleid worms in high abundance up to 7.5 kilometres from the fish farms. Dorvilleid worms are seen as 'reliable indicators' of severe oxygen depletion on the ocean floor. They were found to have 'increased in abundance' in these World Heritage Area waters. The bureaucratic response to this evidence of the destruction of a World Heritage Area ecosystem was to 'cease using' dorvilleid worms as an appropriate indicator species.[20]

Redefining what was evidence of a problem didn't make the problem go away, though. In September 2014

the heads of Huon Aquaculture and Petuna (the third
and smallest Tasmanian salmon farmer) sent an email,
later leaked, to the Tasmanian premier, the minister for
Primary Industries and Water, and a number of senior
bureaucrats, alleging that Tassal 'was about to breach
the biomass cap on Macquarie Harbour, and that the
Tasmanian regulator [EPA] was engaged in disingenu-
ous and misleading conduct and that this was putting
at risk both the health of the waterways and the future
of the industry'.[21]

In 2016, instead of decreasing the number of
salmon, the Tasmanian government agreed to increase
the Macquarie Harbour salmon limit to 21,500
tonnes.[22] Through 2016 and 2017 Tassal and the EPA
tried to blame the deoxygenation on numerous factors
other than salmon farming. By 2017 the deterioration
had grown so extreme that Huon Aquaculture took
the director of the EPA and his minister to court for
not properly regulating Macquarie Harbour. In an
act that shadowed its closeness to politicians and
bureaucrats, Tassal 'entered the case on the side of the
government'.[23]

In February 2017, after the public outrage that
followed revelations in an ABC *Four Corners* episode,
'Big Fish', that a science report had found all marine
fauna within at least a 500-metre radius of a Tassal
salmon lease, close to the World Heritage Area, was

dead, the EPA was finally forced to act. It ordered Tassal to destock salmon leases at Macquarie Harbour.[24] Tassal salmon farms were death zones.

In 2018, the EPA at last announced a reduction in the ceiling of production in Macquarie Harbour to 9500 tonnes. But by then it was too late. Over a million and a quarter salmon had died in consequence of catastrophically low oxygen levels. Worse, wild marine species suffered, most notably the rare maugean skate, only found in Macquarie Harbour.[25] The species is now close to extinction with 'the balance of the evidence' suggesting that it 'is not able to reproduce in the current circumstances in Macquarie Harbour'.[26] The long-term effect on the harbour was to devastate the entire ecosystem, including its World Heritage Area.

A highly critical 2017 University of Tasmania co-authored report, led by conservation ecologist Professor Jamie Kirkpatrick, found that despite salmon industry and government claims to the contrary, the cause of oxygen reduction was salmon farming. According to Professor Kirkpatrick and his co-authors, 'the legal, regulatory and science governance . . . appear to have contributed to serious environmental degradation'. Macquarie Harbour, they concluded, was a case study in which 'pollution from an industry appears to threaten legally recognised national and international natural values.'[27]

Today, remote bays in the World Heritage Area, some distance from the salmon farms, are thick with green filamentous algae and black plastic pollution—the fatal black and green scar of salmon farming.

'There was an abundance of good science, collected by the government itself, that identified the huge risks to the harbour posed by the expansion,' Dr Koehnken told me. 'Now they say we didn't know then. We did know.'

Anywhere other than Tasmania, an environmental disaster on the scale of Macquarie Harbour would have seen a major public investigation or report, top bureaucrats losing their jobs, companies substantially fined and punished, new regimes introduced, new, far more rigorous regulatory codes implemented, CEOs pressured by their boards and politicians in the firing line.

But this was Tasmania, and in Tasmania it was all swept under the carpet so that, amazingly, the industry emerged not only unscathed and unpunished, but resolved on another massive public water grab. This time it was to be Storm Bay, the magnificent waterway between Bruny Island and the Tasman Peninsula. For many Tasmanians it was a case of déjà vu. The greater the crime, the greater the cover-up, and the more bald-faced the next ask, the next take.

As several scientists put it to me, referencing the infamous woodchipping monopoly that devastated Tasmania's internationally unique wildlands through the 1990s and 2000s, poisoning Tasmanian life and corrupting its democracy, salmon farming is the new Gunns.

On the panel, Louise Cherrie repeatedly raised the troubling example of Macquarie Harbour, to no avail. Yet it was the same industry, the same companies, the same lack of rules, the same practices, the same lack of science, the same regulators, and the same key players. Cherrie was told that if Storm Bay was another environmental disaster like Macquarie Harbour, then 'it was on the industry'; how 'if the salmon industry collapsed that was the salmon industry's problem'. Cherrie pointed out that it wasn't just a problem for the industry: the collapse of the industry would mean Tasmanians would lose their jobs, and surely that mattered; Macquarie Harbour might never recover, and if Storm Bay were to suffer a similar fate, surely that mattered, too.

The salmon industry's only answer to the many questions Macquarie Harbour raised was what they termed 'adaptive management'—adapting management as problems arise. 'It means push until it is too late,' says Cherrie, 'and only react after the damage is done.'

Cherrie decided to do her own due diligence. She went to the EPA and asked to see how adaptive management had worked at Macquarie Harbour.

'If the Australian public saw what I saw that day,' Cherrie said, 'they would not be buying salmon.'

She watched footage filmed beneath a salmon farm showing piles of faeces full of long white worms—the dorvilleid worms.

'It looked like it was snowing white worms,' Cherrie recalled, pointing out that while the public is allowed to see video footage from non-impacted marine farming sites, these videos of badly impacted sites are kept highly secret and the public is not allowed to see them. 'Unlike any other food industry, consumers don't see how Tasmanian salmon is made. The community couldn't handle seeing that vision.'

The EPA—after reviewing the footage Cherrie found herself staring at in horror—told the salmon company there was a problem that needed rectifying. And yet eight months later the company had done nothing.

Such was adaptive management. Even when the damage was done, nothing happened. Even when the regulator had the evidence. Nothing. Cherrie was shocked. She had never seen such an absence of proper management by an industry, or such a failure by a regulator to respond. 'You wouldn't get away with any of this in mining,' she said. 'I can't understand how the Tasmanian salmon industry gets away with such negligent practices.'

According to Cherrie, the EPA had the power to force Tassal to act but chose not to push the most powerful corporation in Tasmania. The industry and the government, Cherrie felt, both had a lot of explaining to do.

But there were no explanations. There were no penalties and there was no action. There were just mounds of fish faeces accumulating in Macquarie Harbour. Cherrie explained how a marine ecosystem doesn't readily recover from huge piles of fish faeces crawling with worms. 'It's clear evidence,' she said, 'of a system way out of balance.'

She repeatedly advised the panel that the Storm Bay expansion couldn't be considered without proper scientific modelling and until there was such modelling—which would take some years to complete—there could be no approval. Cherrie says that despite 'clear and known scenarios for environmental harm and fish kills, operational plans to deal with these issues were non-existent or grossly inadequate.' There were no plans for storm events, waste management or net problems.

No heed was paid to the three days of public hearings and submissions. Community concerns were dismissed as irrelevant, despite the risk a lack of social licence presented to the industry.

The panel was adamant: the farm would go in because the minister would approve it anyway. The more Cherrie and Nowak tried to talk on the panel about the science the more they were treated with disdain. To Cherrie and Nowak it was inexplicable that the panel members acted against compelling logic to favour the industrial option.

When the two women scientists began to ask more questions and demanded to see more detail, their role on the panel came under attack. A senior government officer had to sit in on the final meeting simply to ensure Cherrie had her opinions heard. Panel members 'were either openly dismissive of Nowak and Cherrie's concerns or silent'. When Cherrie kept asking questions, she was told 'it was too late'.[28] They had to approve the gigantic expansion: the salmon companies were already growing salmon for deployment in Storm Bay.

Unable to halt the expansion, the two women scientists tried to effect small, responsible changes. Based on best practice elsewhere and citing numerous scientific studies, Professor Nowak argued that because of biosecurity rights there should be a *minimum* five-kilometre buffer zone between the proposed fish farms. A reduced buffer zone meant more fish farms, but it also meant a greatly increased risk of disease transfer. When told that if the farms were five kilometres apart a third farm would not be viable, Cherrie said, 'Then it's not viable.' The buffer zone was nevertheless reduced to four kilometres.[29]

Cherrie, who prides herself on being a pragmatist who in her work with resource and heavy industries finds constructive outcomes, recalls that it was 'the only time in my professional life I felt I couldn't make a difference'.

Appearing before a confidential session of the Legislative Council's Fin Fish Farming Inquiry in 2020, some details of which later became available in a heavily redacted Right to Information document, Professor Nowak said she was told by one panel member 'that the industry can't be controlled'. She went on to decry 'an independent panel where the public believes there are independent people when they are not'. At the same session, Cherrie said that the process ensured approval: 'Because they [the salmon companies] had made the application, they will get approved.'[30]

Professor Nowak, an industry veteran, concluded that the panel was 'a waste of taxpayers' money', later telling me it was than 'a complete rubber stamp' for the salmon industry.

When Professor Nowak and Louise Cherrie announced they would resign, a government official told them they weren't allowed to. They resigned anyway, Professor Nowak saying she wouldn't have been able to live with herself had she stayed on. Far from being best practice, they wrote to the minister, the panel showed 'an undue propensity to support what is operationally convenient for the aquaculture industry'.[31]

The government refused to release their resignation letter.

What Louise Cherrie and Barbara Nowak's experience seems to suggest is that it was all a done deal: that the Storm Bay decision had been made long before, not by public process but by private salmon corporations; and that the panel on which they sat was structured by legislation to answer not to parliament but to the salmon corporations' need for profit. If this is so, the panel existed merely as window dressing to give the appearance of due process and probity where there was none.

The panel charged with reviewing proposed fish farms and making 'recommendations to the minister in respect of draft plans, draft modifications and draft amendments' could only recommend the largest industrial development in recent Tasmanian history go ahead along the lines the salmon industry wanted. At the least, this shows the whole byzantine regulatory framework cited as world's best practice is no more than an elaborate lie. At the worst, it suggests that no matter the evidence, no matter the concerns, no matter the science, no matter the history, no matter the consequences, the governance of the industry is run in knowing bad faith by a Tasmanian government in curious servitude to the greed of the salmon corporations.

And so, ignoring the lessons of Macquarie Harbour, rejecting advice about possible heavy metal contamination, lacking a social licence, and in the absence of scientific modelling without any adequate baseline scientific studies, against the advice of two of its principal scientists, who had resigned in protest, in the face of widespread community opposition, the panel recommended to the minister that the massive expansion of salmon farming into Storm Bay be approved.

Documents recently obtained by the ABC now reveal it did so in a meeting in which only three sitting members were present. With Cherrie and Nowak having quit, it had to rely on the votes of two members whose terms had expired to make its quorum of five—a move without ethical basis and of dubious legality.[32]

In a final sordid twist, to complete the lie of proper process and as if to drive home the powerlessness of the women, the power of the salmon industry and the cravenness of the Tasmanian government, Cherrie and Nowak discovered that without their permission their names had been added to the approval decision.

3

IF WE ARE WHAT WE EAT, WHAT OUR FOOD has eaten in turn matters. Yet it's easier to find out what you're feeding your dog than what you're feeding yourself when you eat Tasmanian salmon.

Should you search the murky filth of a salmon pen to discover what constitutes the millions of feed pellets that drift down, you would quickly find yourself enveloped in a growing darkness. A veil of secrecy, green-washed and flesh-pink-rosetted, was long ago drawn over the methods and practices of the Tasmanian salmon industry, from its inexplicable influence over government processes to its grotesque environmental impacts. But the biggest secret of all is what the industry feeds its salmon.

From the beginning, the outsized environmental damage the industrial production of Tasmanian salmon creates has been outsourced to where it can't be seen—under water—and to countries so far-off few have any idea that the problems and suffering of these countries are connected to the Tasmanian salmon industry.

In the early decades of farming, Tasmanian salmon—a carnivore in the wild—were largely fed on anchovy-based fishmeal and fish oil imported from Peru.[33] The fishmeal industry on which the rise of the 'clean and green' Tasmanian salmon industry was built left the sea surrounding Peru's capital of anchovy fishing, Chimbote, contaminated, its coastline badly degraded and the town seriously polluted. According to Professor Romulo Loayza, a biology professor at the National University of Santa in Nuevo Chimbote, there are around 53 million cubic metres of sludge in the seas around Chimbote, residual waste from the fishmeal factories, which in some parts reach more than two metres in height.[34]

In an investigation for the *Guardian*, Andrew Wasley observed that the Chimbote fishmeal factories' insatiable demand for anchovy 'impacted on the sea's natural food chain, and reduced stocks of previously plentiful species fished for human consumption'. He describes Chimbote in 2008 with black smoke billowing from the fishmeal factories drifting through the streets, 'obscuring vision and choking passers-by. It looked like the aftermath of a bomb.' In 'one poor community ... more than a dozen women and children gathered in the dusty, unpaved street to vent their anger at pollution from the fishmeal plants: they claimed they were responsible for asthma, bronchial and skin problems, particularly in children.'[35]

The protesting Peruvian women and their sick children is one image of Tasmanian salmon that won't appear in any glossy history of the industry's rapid rise or its marketing of itself as environmentally responsible. Nor will that of the sea lions slaughtered by local anchovy fishermen, who saw them as competitors for a dwindling resource, their corpses scattered along a rubbish-strewn Chimbote beach, 'quietly rotting in the sunshine'.[36]

Today, Tassal claims it uses 1.73 kilograms of wild fish to make one kilogram of salmon.[37] In other words, a lot more protein to make a lot less. Yet a major study found that 90 per cent of fish caught globally that were not used for human consumption were 'food-grade or prime food-grade fish'.[38]

Fishmeal and fish oil are the products of global supply chains of staggering complexity and opacity, subject to constant change because of weather, natural catastrophe and politics; captive to a thriving black market in which fishmeal from one country with unacceptable practices can be illegally traded to another and then on-sold as that second country's product.

A recent report by the Netherlands-based Changing Markets Foundation linked leading global fish-feed giants BioMar and Skretting—which, along with Ridley, are the feed suppliers to Tasmania's salmon industry—to 'illegal and unsustainable fishing practices' that were 'accelerating the collapse of local fish stocks', 'driving illegal, unregulated and unreported fishing' and 'wreaking environmental damage around production sites'.[39]

The salmon industry rejects such reports, claiming that its fishmeal and oil are legitimately and ethically sourced.[40] It points to the fishmeal industry's certification standard, known as the International Fishmeal and Fish Oil Organization Global Standard for Responsible Supply (IFFO RS)—IFFO being the fishmeal producers' own global association. Or it was, until last year when, in the wake of the Changing Markets Foundation report and subsequent controversy, it was rebranded as the MarinTrust Standard to distance itself from IFFO. Accordingly, the IFFO MarinTrust Standard has been condemned as 'a sustainability smokescreen'.[41] If the standard is not independent, as its critics claim, it's difficult to believe it is trustworthy, given the conflict of interest.

Salmon farming is about creating protein by stealing it from others. Far from being a sustainable solution to the global collapse of wild fishing stocks, fish farming is driving overfishing, with an estimated 25 per cent of fish caught globally being used for aquaculture. Alassane

Samba, the former head of research at Senegal's Oceanic Research Institute, has warned that depleting fish at the bottom of the food chain 'could lead to a collapse of the marine ecosystem'.[42] In at least one case, a Namibian sardinella fishery, that nightmare is already reality, with the fishery collapsing entirely and the void left by the sardinella being filled with jellyfish—the first case in the world where fish were replaced with jellyfish.[43] More salmon for us means less food for others. Far from feeding the world today, Tasmanian salmon corporations are thieving from its future.

This may not worry those who love to eat salmon. But what may concern them is the way fishmeal and fish oil is transported. Unless stabilised with chemicals, fishmeal and fish oil go rancid, losing their precious omega-3 oils—the source of salmon's much-vaunted health-food status. The chemical stabiliser of choice is ethoxyquin.

Developed by Monsanto in the 1950s as a pesticide,[44] manufactured from petrochemicals, with a range of uses including preventing rubber cracking,[45] ethoxyquin also ensures fishmeal won't self-combust in transport, leading the International Maritime Organization to stipulate it as one of two obligatory fishmeal stabilisers to prevent fires and explosions.[46]

Skretting, the largest salmon feed producer in Tasmania, supplying both Tassal and Petuna, replying to questions put to them in March 2021, said their feeds 'are well within' European limits of 150 mg of ethoxyquin per kilogram of feed. According to Skretting, 'In Australia and New Zealand, ethoxyquin is considered generally regarded [sic] as safe.' Neither BioMar nor Ridley answered questions about ethoxyquin, and their websites are silent on the petrochemical-based additive.

It has been known for some decades that ethoxyquin could 'lead to cancer in exposed animals'.[47] Ethoxyquin has been shown to cross the blood–brain barrier of animals, can accumulate in the fatty tissue of humans, lead to chromosome breakage and is detectable in human breast milk.[48] The eminent Dutch toxicologist Hendrik Tennekes suspected that ethoxyquin could influence the brain development of human foetuses.[49]

The major source of ethoxyquin contamination of humans would appear to be aquaculture: a 2013 Polish study found that 'farmed fish is probably the major source of EQ [ethoxyquin] and its residues for European consumers'.[50] Research funded by the Norwegian Seafood Research Fund and major global salmon feed companies, including BioMar and Skretting, concluded that ethoxyquin 'was detected in salmon fillets regardless of the amount contained in the feed'.[51]

Victoria Bohne, a Norwegian scientist assigned by Norway's prestigious National Institute of Nutrition and Seafood Research to research ethoxyquin, made

European headlines in 2015 when she admitted on German television that she no longer dared to eat farmed salmon because of ethoxyquin.[52]

According to Professor Edmund Maser of the Department of Toxicology and Pharmacology at the University of Kiel, ethoxyquin 'can be mutagenic and toxic. You need to eat a lot of farmed salmon to reach those levels, but people who eat a lot of salmon can reach them. Also, think of children and people with less body weight, for them the limit is lower. My answer is that one must find alternatives.'[53]

After a series of studies associated the chemical with a range of human health issues, in 2017 the EU banned the use of ethoxyquin as a food additive, and its use in human food is similarly banned in Australia.[54] But the majority of Tasmanian salmon continues to be produced using feed containing ethoxyquin.

And so, to get salmon's supposed health benefits, Australian salmon consumers have for more than three decades also been consuming ethoxyquin residue. Just as they were never confronted with images of the devastation of places like Chimbote, nor were consumers informed that the salmon they ate came tainted with the carcinogen used to transport the fishmeal and fish oil, along with PCBs and heavy metals that were concentrated in the smaller fish species used to make that fishmeal and oil.

'Marine feed ingredients,' drily observes one scientific paper analysing alternative salmon feed ingredients, 'traditionally used in commercial fish feeds, are the source of ... persistent organic pollutants (POPs) such as polychlorinated biphenyls (PCBs), dioxins and furans (PCDD/Fs), organochlorine pesticides (OCPs), and polybrominated diphenyl ethers (PBDEs), as well as elements such as arsenic, mercury, cadmium, lead, copper, zinc and fluorine.'[55]

With ethoxyquin being kept secret from Australian consumers, the only problem the Tasmanian salmon industry had with fishmeal was cost. Fishmeal is expensive, and with salmon feed half the cost of growing salmon, any reduction in the amount of fishmeal used in salmon feed meant a reduction in production cost. And so over the last twenty years the Tasmanian salmon industry has sought to make feed cheaper by lessening the amount of fishmeal in it and sourcing protein from other food streams.

While the change from a salmon diet that was principally fishmeal-based to principally plant- and land animal-based meant the amount of ethoxyquin, POPs, PCBs and heavy metals in farmed salmon was reduced, it created several new problems. In the wake of mad cow disease—a fatal illness to humans consequent on feeding animals other dead animals—the use of discarded remnants of butchered cows, sheep and poultry in aquaculture feeds was banned in Europe. Yet in Australia it remained legal to feed remnants of slaughtered cows, sheep and chickens to salmon—so that's what the Tasmanian salmon industry does.

The majority of the animal protein used in Tasmanian salmon feed is chicken-based. According to Skretting, 30.4 per cent of their annual total ingredients for salmon feed is chicken-derived—10.96 per cent is poultry oil, 14.92 per cent poultry meal, and 4.52 per cent feather meal. Chicken meal was legally defined in 2015 as 'prepared from . . . the carcass of slaughtered poultry, such as heads, feet, intestines and frames'.[56] A 2016 report by the Australian Renderers Association found that 'foreign matter in poultry material can also include plucker fingers, aluminium bag clips and elastic netting/bands'.[57] Plastic and metal, in other words, amid the macerated brains, ground-up feathers, mashed-up beaks, claws and guts of battery hens.

Would those who think they are making an ethical choice buying Tasmanian salmon do so if they knew much of it is reconstituted from the waste streams flowing from the industrial butchering of chickens?

Another way of replacing fishmeal in salmons' diet is to use high-protein vegetable matter such as lupins, wheat, canola and soy. Much of this comes from Australian farms—except soy, the wonder bean high in protein, which is sourced through global supply chains from South America.

In late 2018 the three major global fish-feed companies—two of which, Skretting and BioMar, supply the overwhelming bulk of Tasmanian salmon feed—were rocked by a scandal exposed in leading Norwegian newspaper *Dagbladet*. Brazilian soy suppliers to their Norwegian operations were 'linked to slave-like working conditions, violent conflicts over land, illegal deforestation, the use of illegal pesticides and soy grown in indigenous territories'.[58]

Illegal deforestation to create new soy farms in South America, particularly in the Amazon and Cerrado, is deeply embedded in the rise of the salmon industry globally and throws a long shadow over any attempt by the local industry to present salmon as a green product. Skretting has acknowledged that 'soybean cultivation is one of the main commodities driving deforestation ... [which] will lead to less carbon fixation from the atmosphere and increased climate change'.[59] BioMar, in its most recent Sustainability Report, admits that 'soy cultivation can lead to adverse environmental outcomes such as deforestation ... the native habitat for a variety of species is destroyed and the carbon stored within the vegetation is released'. Far from denying that its soy is coming from deforested areas, BioMar seems to acknowledge that it possibly does, saying that 'with deforestation being a problem in many countries . . . average [carbon] emissions [of its soy meal] are often quite high'.[60]

In Europe, where consumer awareness of the link between salmon and the soy-driven destruction of the Amazon is far greater, the salmon industry and its feed producers are painfully aware of the brand damage this creates with both consumers and investors. Salmon feed suppliers have attempted to clean up their supply chains and improve traceability by working with third-party certification organisations like ProTerra. Much has been improved, particularly in the wake of the *Dagbladet* scandal, which showed good intentions didn't always guarantee good outcomes. But the scale and complexity of soy production in South America means full traceability remains a holy grail rather than an actual achievement.

At the same time, the demand for soy is huge. The massive global explosion in industrial animal production—including salmon—has driven the search for new land for plantations. To give just one example: the planned five-fold increase in Norwegian salmon farming will require the farming of an area of Brazil greater in size than all land in agricultural use in Norway today.[61]

As global demand for soy soars, to clean up one area of its production is not necessarily to improve the whole—often the opposite. It pushes elsewhere dirty soy production, with all its grotesque, interrelated horrors—slavery, forced labour, indigenous dispossession, massive chemical fertiliser and pesticide regimes, destruction of globally unique forests, megafires, to say nothing of the extraordinary impacts on global heating.[62] A good example is global food giant and soy supplier Cargill, which, while a major supplier of ProTerra-certified soy to salmon feed companies, 'continues to be linked to Amazon deforestation'.[63]

The salmon feed companies' only answer to this gigantic, complex global problem is certification, which it parades as a guarantee of the environmental and social worth of its soy. But on closer inspection certification is a dirty piece of glass that shatters when it's touched.

In reply to questions on this subject in March 2021, Skretting Australia wrote that their Brazilian 'imported soya protein concentrate has been ProTerra certified since 2016 ... The requirement in the ProTerra standard is that soya cannot come from agricultural land that has been cleared for cultivation.'

That requirement is not always easily met. A comprehensive 2019 report commissioned by the Netherlands International Union for Conservation of Nature concluded that governments of soy-importing countries that 'seek to avoid deforestation' needed to take regulatory action. The reliance of voluntary soy-certification standards, including ProTerra, 'on local legal compliance in most producers' countries is not enough to avoid a considerable amount of potential deforestation ... without a good level of assurance, deforestation-free soy can never be guaranteed.'[64] According to a major report on soy use in the Norwegian salmon industry by the respected Rainforest Foundation Norway, ProTerra has been criticised for lacking transparency and independent verification, creating 'major obstacles when trying to ascertain whether the scheme actually ensures that certified soya is sustainably produced'. The report goes on to say, 'The criteria are not good enough, allowing the deforestation of partially-degraded forest and allowing soya growers to be certified even if they use dangerous pesticides, so long as they have plans to reduce usage.'[65]

Even with ProTerra certification, it was 'impossible for consumers and others to know whether the cultivation of soya used in Norwegian farmed salmon has contributed to deforestation or the hazardous use of pesticides'—a conclusion that applies equally to Australian consumers and Tasmanian salmon fed on certified Brazilian soy.[66]

In 2018 Skretting admitted there is 'difficulty in being certain that all suppliers to our own suppliers operate in a responsible, legal way'.[67] Skretting's acknowledgement—that certified soy products may violate their obligations to act responsibly—would

seem tantamount to an admission that its fish feed
was still being produced in illegal and highly damaging
ways to the local and global environment as well as
to communities, despite ProTerra certification. Its
commitments—couched in qualifications—sound
more aspirational than real: soybean farms 'should
also respect social and human rights, while the farm-
land should not be illegally deforested land'.[68] Yet, by
its own admission, in its 2019 sustainability report,
to which Skretting referred me, the company did not
have 'a regular and mandatory system to trace soy
products back to the country or region of soybean
cultivation', and only 33 per cent of its soy purchases
met the criteria of being deforestation-free.[69] All of
which is less than comforting to anyone who thinks
Tasmanian salmon is good for the environment.

BioMar Australia, when asked, did not detail where
their soy came from, instead referring to two documents: its sourcing policy and its 2019 Sustainability
Report. Though BioMar boasts of its transparency,
and the traceability of its soy, its provenance is neither
traceable nor transparent to the layperson. It is in
essence an act of trust on the part of the consumer to
believe BioMar's claims.

The BioMar sourcing policy only voices the aspira-
tion that 'BioMar has a programme seeking to eliminate
use of raw materials causing deforestation of tropical

rainforests within 2020.' Beyond stating that and its soy's ProTerra certification, it says BioMar supported 'the current activities of the Round Table on Responsible Soy (RTRS), which seeks to promote the use of a standard to ensure that large scale production of soya in South America is undertaken in a responsible manner relative to ecological, social and economic criteria'.[70]

If by South America BioMar means Argentina, there the demand for new soy farms has also led to major deforestation, particularly in the vast Gran Chaco forest—twice the area of California and second only to the Amazon in size and biodiversity, and now plagued with similar problems: land clearing, the displacement of indigenous peoples, and extreme environmental damage.[71] But it seems no one can say with certainty whether a BioMar Australia salmon-fed pellet contains soy from Brazil or Uruguay or Argentina.

The major global salmon feed companies are seeking to clean up their act and the acts of their suppliers, but it is a difficult, perhaps ultimately impossible task. This may explain why they cannot trust the consumer with the full truth of the failure of their good intentions. The reality on the ground is problematic and complex, something even their own executives, seeking change, acknowledge.

As BioMar's sustainability specialist, Erik Olav Gracey, said in 2019 after visiting Brazil to investigate

BioMar's supply chains there in the wake of the *Dagbladet* scandal, 'The effective enforcement and implementation of key legislation by government agencies is hampered by the sheer size of the country, unstable political climate, and lack of resources in key areas.'

'You can see,' Gracey said, 'that there is ample room for improvement ... we are sourcing agricultural commodities that may be in conflict with natural vegetation and forest.'[72]

As forest and native vegetation loss accelerates in Brazil, the issue of the sourcing of soy has become such a public relations problem for a panicked European salmon industry that late in 2020 major salmon producers, salmon feed companies (including BioMar) and retailers publicly called on six of the world's largest commodity traders 'to up their efforts on Brazilian deforestation' and 'end soy driven deforestation'.[73] Such efforts are laudable and not to be dismissed. But it is also true that for as long as salmon consumption increases and soy remains a key ingredient of salmon, so too will the demand for soy grow and so too will pressure grow for more land for other soy cultivation, and so salmon will continue to drive deforestation.

Approximately 80 per cent of soy grown in the world is for industrial animal- and fish-feed production. Between 2009 and 2018, global soybean production increased by 38 per cent and the land cultivated for soy grew to 123 million hectares. By 2028 it is projected to be 151 million hectares. Most of that growth is expected to happen in Brazil, where it is likely to drive further deforestation, violence, land conflicts and global heating.[74] These crimes will only be halted when we reduce our soy consumption. And that can only happen if we reduce our consumption of industrially produced beef, pork, chicken—and salmon.

The situation is perhaps beyond remedy; certainly, some of the smaller European salmon-feed companies, such as Danish Aller Aqua, think so. In 2021 it withdrew completely from sourcing soy in South America and switched to European soy producers. 'The deforestation issue has been an increasing concern, not least during 2020,' Aller Aqua group vice-president Henrik T. Halken was quoted as saying. Locally sourced soy carried the additional virtue of reducing CO_2 emissions by 41 per cent.[75]

Such is the interconnection of opaque global supply chains that by buying a fillet of the supposed environmentally friendly Tasmanian salmon, a Sydney or Melbourne consumer may be lighting the very flame that burns yet more of the Amazon and the Gran Chaco, daily heating up our world a little more.

But this is only the beginning of the bad news.

By altering a carnivore's diet to one that includes ever larger amounts of plant-based protein, the nutritional profile of salmon has been fundamentally altered for the worse.

Tasmanian salmon's omega-3 oils—the main nutritional argument for eating it—are only obtainable from the fishmeal and fish oil the salmon eat. As the proportion of wild-fish derivatives they were fed decreased, so too did the level of omega-3 oils in the salmon decrease by between 30 and 50 per cent with,[76] concluded a 2016 study by the University of Stirling's Institute of Aquaculture into the similarly altered diet of Scottish-farmed salmon, 'some compromise of the nutritional benefit to the human consumer'.[77] Comparing Scottish salmon from 2006 to those farmed in 2015, the Scottish scientists found that you would need to eat 'a double portion' in 2015 to achieve the same omega-3 levels of a single portion eaten nine years earlier.

If consumers think Tasmanian salmon is good for them, it may only be half as good for you today as it used to be—or even worse. For the increasing use of plant-based food sources has also changed the fish's fatty acid profile, significantly increasing the amount of omega-6 oils—the so-called 'bad' fats. In consequence, those who buy Tasmanian salmon as a heart food are also eating fats that are bad for them. Even worse, the higher the amount of omega-6 oils, the less able the body is to absorb the already greatly reduced omega-3 oils.[78] In other words, the increased omega-6 fats in

Tasmanian salmon cancel out much of the value of the already reduced omega-3 oils.

And the science suggests that this has health consequences.

One study showed that feeding mice salmon fillets with a high omega-6 to low omega-3 fatty acid ratio led to weight gain and tissue inflammation.[79] According to Dr Giovanni Turchini, a professor of nutrition and food science at Deakin University, an imbalance between the two types of fatty acids means 'we put our body in a constant inflammation mode and that can facilitate a lot of diseases'.[80] Those include cardiovascular disease, diabetes and some forms of cancer.

When you strip away all the arguments for industrially produced salmon, advocates of Big Salmon retreat to one: that if you wish to feed the world, you must support the salmon industry as the most efficient way of producing animal protein. 'With 821 million people worldwide going to bed hungry each night,' Huon Aquaculture declaims on its website page *How to be an ethical consumer*, 'exploration and expansion into aquaculture is a necessary step for sustainable protein sources into the future'.[81]

This argument crumbles under closer inspection: when grains that could be fed to humans are fed to animals instead, to produce meat, as little as 10 per cent of the energy contained in the grains is converted into edible protein. When that animal protein in turn is fed to salmon, you have further losses.[82] If you were serious about feeding the world—and genuinely concerned for its health—you would give the people loaves and hummus, not a salmon cutlet.

And that is because Tasmanian salmon production is not food production so much as part of a highly industrialised global system of food *reduction* to make profit. Justified as a solution to feeding the world into the future, the truth of salmon farming in Tasmania is the exact opposite: the theft of food from the poor, the commons from the people, and the future from the young, to please affluent consumers and profit big business.[83]

Everyone else loses.

Yet the only problem arising from Tasmanian salmon's diet of chemicals, crushed chicken skulls, beaks and feathers, along with wild fish pillaged from distant oceans and soy meal of dubious, perhaps criminal provenance that would seem to concern the Tasmanian industry is this: the unpalatable grey flesh industrially produced salmon has in consequence.

For this reason, the industry in its earliest days in Norway sold its product as 'ivory salmon'. When that marketing ploy failed, producers fed salmon a synthetic red dye called astaxanthin to artificially replicate the red-coloured flesh wild salmon acquire from eating small crustaceans. From that time on, the industry has dyed its salmon for one reason only: to make its highly manipulated product look like wild fish that consumers would buy.

Just as you use colour swatches to choose house paint, the salmon corporations use colour swatches to choose their salmon's colour. DSM, the manufacturer of the SalmoFan™ colour swatch chart, claims to be 'the industry standard across the world for measuring salmon fillet color'. An article headlined 'Fake-Nature' observes, 'With the help of the SalmoFan's color swatches, the farmers can decide when their product is blush enough for market. Consumers prefer a deeper shade, with 66% choosing color No. 33.'[84]

Getting No. 33 right is a matter of commercial life or death, as Ridley, the fish-feed manufacturer, found out in 2017 when it took Huon Aquaculture to court after Huon refused to pay Ridley $17.5 million for fish feed. Huon's refusal stemmed from its claim that Ridley fish pellets failed to include sufficient pigment, 'causing production of fish with poor flesh colour'. This led to 'loss of sales . . . compensation claims by customers, and loss of reputation', Huon said in court documents.[85]

In the wake of bad publicity from the devastating 2016 *Four Corners* report into the Macquarie Harbour disaster, Tassal publicly announced it was moving away from using synthetic astaxanthin to dye salmon to a natural pigment, and Huon Aquaculture followed, saying it was also transitioning.[86] For a period after 2017, Huon did experiment with a natural astaxanthin, marketed as Panaferd. But, like so much else with the secretive salmon industry, these announcements smack more of marketing than truth. Four years later most, perhaps all, of Tasmanian salmon's grey flesh is dyed pink with synthetic astaxanthin. And that's unsurprising given that while synthetic astaxanthin can be as much as 20 per cent of the total cost of salmon feed, natural astaxanthin—at US$7000 a kilogram—is more than triple the cost of synthetic astaxanthin, which costs US$2000 a kilogram.[87]

In reply to written questions in March 2021, Tassal and Petuna were forthright in admitting they use synthetic astaxanthin. Huon Aquaculture, which in 2019 told the Legislative Council Inquiry into Fin Fish Farming it was using natural dye,[88] has two years later become mute on its choice of pigment: on repeatedly being asked if Huon uses synthetic astaxanthin, the company referred to their website, which offers no clarity on the matter, and to the websites of their feed suppliers, not one of which addresses the question of whether the supplier uses synthetic or natural astax-anthin. Nor did the feed supplier websites—for all their talk of transparency—satisfactorily address many of the other pressing questions about salmon feed that one might reasonably expect should be a simple matter of public record.

With chutzpah typical of its promotion of its synthetic fish product, Tassal describes synthetic astaxanthin as 'a pure version of what is eaten by wild salmon, this is why we refer to it as nature-identical'.[89] In advertising targeted at women, the company claims that astaxanthin is 'a powerful anti-oxidant that effectively slows down the aging process by protecting cells against harmful free radicals thus reducing "invisible swelling"'.[90]

However, the 'nature-identical' synthetic astaxanthin that makes salmon 'so much better for your health, and for your skin' turns out to be made from petrochemicals. It would only be a pure version of what wild salmon eat if wild salmon drank oil distillates.

The much-touted health-giving properties of astaxanthin are derived from studies of natural astaxanthin, found in wild salmon, crabs and crayfish. But synthetic astaxanthin, as fed to Tasmanian salmon, was found in a 2013 study to be fifty times weaker than natural astaxanthin in 'singlet oxygen quenching' and approximately twenty times weaker 'in free radical elimination'. This 'extreme difference in antioxidant activity' was described as 'quite profound'.[91]

As well as synthetic astaxanthin possibly containing 'trace amounts of residual solvents and chemical reagents', the differences between synthetic astaxanthin (S-AX) and natural astaxanthin (N-AX) led the study authors to conclude that 'although both [are] called "astaxanthin" [they] must be considered completely different substances'.[92] In other words, the fish farmers' petrochemical dye has nowhere near the health benefits obtained when you eat wild, naturally pigmented salmon.

Not only that, but the synthetic dye, far from being a guarantee of good health, raises health questions. The authors of the study recommended 'against the use of S-AX as a human nutraceutical supplement until extensive, long-term safety parameters have been established and human clinical trials have been conducted'. The study raised a series of questions as 'to the safety and potential health benefits of S-AX.'[93] Synthetic astaxanthin is *only* approved by the United States Food and Drug Administration and the European Food Safety Authority as a feed additive in aquaculture, while a 2020 study found that natural forms of astaxanthin 'are now preferred for human consumption' as supplements.[94]

None of this has stopped the marketers of Tasmanian salmon from making ever more astonishing claims for the health benefits of eating dyed salmon. Huon Aquaculture claims it will 'not only keep you healthy but also keep you looking good',[95] improving everything from heart health to joint pain, as well as raising the prospect of its being able to treat cancer, and improving male fertility.[96] To take the last wild claim as an example to serve for all: this seems to refer to a highly limited, never replicated 2005 study of only thirty men[97] that, in any case, used AstaCarox, a natural astaxanthin.[98]

If all this wasn't troubling enough, there is the industry's abuse of antibiotics. The dangers of anti-biotic abuse in aquaculture have long been a cause for concern. A 1992 cholera outbreak in Ecuador was linked by scientists to antibiotic use in the shrimp-farming industry.[99] Scientific studies are clear on the dangers of the practice and yet an industry that says it answers to science ignores it, risking the health of both its workers and its consumers. A report into the use of the antibiotic oxytetracycline in Chilean salmon farms found these farms could 'play important roles as reservoirs of bacteria carrying genetic determinants for high-level tetracycline resistance, prompting an important risk to public health for workers involved in fish culturing and processing'.[100]

Even low levels of antibiotics found in farmed salmon (marketed as antibiotic-free) in the US have been linked, in an Arizona State University study, to the growth of antibiotic resistance in the human population.[101] An international study by infectious diseases experts expressed specific concern about how the use of antibiotics in aquaculture could create drug-resistant bacteria and transferable resistant genes that 'may reach humans directly' and how 'efforts are needed . . . to reduce the risk to human health', including regulatory control and regular monitoring.[102] Even Russia—a country not celebrated for its public health initiatives—showed more concern for its consumers than the Tasmanian authorities when it recently placed restrictions on the imports of Chilean salmon after discovering traces of oxytetracycline in farmed salmon.[103]

Yet, in spite of the dangers it presents to the Australian and Asian public, Tasmanian regulators tolerate antibiotic abuse in the state's salmon farming. Given the global nature of the antibiotic resistance crisis, given the World Health Organization has for several years recommended antibiotics should not be routinely used in animal farming,[104] it would be reasonable to expect that their use in Tasmanian salmon farming—were it world's best practice as the industry and the state government so frequently boast it is—would be non-existent or, at worst, highly regulated and rarely used. Yet this is very far from the case.

Fish disease can be controlled through lower stocking levels and other methods. Huon Aquaculture claims it has not used antibiotics in its sea pens since 2016, or its hatcheries since 2019.[105] But less crowded pens are less profitable, and Tassal, the salmon industry giant and Australia's largest salmon producer, is notorious in the industry for overstocking to the point of the environmental disaster that unfolded in Macquarie Harbour. The cheap, easy way to deal with disease brought on by summer heat and overcrowded pens is antibiotics. And so as temperatures rise so too does Tassal's antibiotic use. In its deeply cynical fashion, despite repeated promises that it was phasing out antibiotics, Tassal *quadrupled* their use between 2012 and 2016, feeding 9.8 grams per tonne of fish, an increase of 353 per cent on the figures three years previously.[106] In 2019 Tassal used 62.28 grams of antibiotics per tonne of salmon—an extraordinary total of more than two tonnes of antibiotics being used in that year alone.[107]

As well as the implications of these rises for farm-workers and consumers, fish do not easily metabolise antibiotics. It is estimated that they excrete 75 per cent of the antibiotics they are given, which then enter marine and river ecosystems, dumped in waterways popular with swimmers and recreational fishermen. Along with this is the uneaten medicated feed, which leaches antibiotics, leading to 'the accumulation of antibiotic residues in the aquatic environment especially in marine sediments, where they can persist for months'.[108]

Because much of the antibiotic use is during the salmon's smolt stage, a lot of the excess is entering the drinking-water catchment of Hobart and the Huon Valley. And yet neither government nor industry study the possible impacts on the marine and riverine ecosystems, far less on the source of most of the drinking water for half Tasmania's population. Consumers, workers and the general public are left unknowing, unwise and unprotected by Tasmanian government regulators, who choose again and again to look the other way.

And so we discover that a food product marketed as capable of treating cancer, of miraculously increasing male virility and restoring women's beauty, is in reality a compound of synthetic dye, antibiotics, petrochemical derivatives, the macerated remains of battery hen beaks, skulls, claws, guts and feathers once destined for abattoir waste streams, along with fishmeal made from jeopardised fish stocks stabilised with a pesticide also used to stop car tyres cracking that happens to be a carcinogen, and soy meal that has possible links to slave labour and the deforestation of the Amazon and the destruction of the Cerrado and that drives global heating.

What salmon actually eat is, finally, what we eat when we eat Tasmanian salmon: secrets and lies.

4

ONE OF THE GREAT FEATS OF TWENTIETH-
century humanity was its industrialisation of food.
What had been artisanal and human and animal-scaled
was maxxed up to match machines, systems and corporate ledgers. The farming of animals became protein
production and protein production became highly
specialised, densely stocked operations on a gigantic
scale, no longer run by individual farmers but by large
corporations with the capital to invest in such industrial
complexes. Beginning in the US with poultry in the
1930s, the aim of these companies was to maximise
output and minimise cost. They would come to rely on
specially formulated feeds, technology, pharmaceuti-
cals, a deskilled, exploited workforce and the systematic
destruction of animals' quality of life in factories where
they were reduced to an industrial product.

As protein became cheaper and more widely available than at any time in human history, chickens, cows

and pigs were reduced to living in ghettos of horror and torment. The fate of industrialised animals whose populations now outweighed any other living form by a massive factor became one of the great environmental and ethical questions of the age. Slowly it grew apparent that the impacts on animals also increasingly affected the labourers on these farms. Working in often wretched, brutal conditions, they and their communities were now prey to everything from pathogens to poisoning to toxic chemicals to zoonotic diseases to water contamination and pandemic outbreaks.[109] And beyond them, more generally, the raft of environmental and food-borne hazards that affected all human beings grew.

By the time salmon farming was invented in Norway in the early 1970s, the industrial model was well and truly established. Almost from the beginning aquaculture was *aquaindustry*. But because the cruelties and crimes of the salmon industry were mostly under water, unseen, almost invisible, Atlantic salmon could be marketed as pure and pristine. The great, enduring paradox was that the more people turned away from industrial land-based protein, the more they embraced industrial *sea*-based protein. Unlike poultry farms—hideous, hell-like bunkers—salmon farms were all grand fjords and glistening seas. What, it seemed, could be more natural and healthier than fish raised in the sea?

And yet the difference between a battery hen and a farmed salmon was only a perception invented by marketing. A Tasmanian Atlantic salmon *is* the battery hen of the sea—or worse: these majestic creatures are perhaps better described as the battery eagle or the battery lion of the sea. For Atlantic salmon are highly developed, complex animals, travelling thousands of kilometres in migration, capable of diving to 700 metres in depth, and of using the Earth's magnetic fields in ways that are poorly understood, finding their way back home to the river, and sometimes their very birthing place, to spawn, famously leaping up rapids and waterfalls to do so. There they make shallow nests, known as redds, in gravel, in which they lay their eggs and then bury them, before repeating the whole epic cycle up to three times before dying. Revered in many cultures, they exist in that realm of special creatures to which we accord respect, and reserved for them is an adjective used for but a handful of other creatures: *noble*. Which only makes their contemporary fate as industrial fodder all the more tragic.

Fish farms are falsely named. In reality, they are gigantic floating feedlots. Even that image is inadequate to convey the cruelty of an industrial system in which lots are stacked one on top of the other in towers of up to 20 metres in height, down which faeces and urine rain. A horizontal cattle feedlot, or even a live-export ship, is a less horrific proposition than a tower block with neither floors nor ceilings. The water in which salmon are condemned to the most wretched of lives is a soup of shit and ammonia. Aggression is common, with hierarchies unable to be established, and cannibalism not unknown.

Sold as clean, green and healthy, no one sees the Atlantic salmon condemned to live and frequently die in these toxic toilets, in which crowded fish ceaselessly circle in giant columns. The salmon, some chromosomally distorted to the point of intense deformity and lifelong pain, are compelled to inhabit water at times so low in oxygen that they choke to death. The image of thousands of cows slowly suffocating to death in a smog-polluted shed would be unacceptable. The reality of thousands of salmon slowly suffocating to death on a hot day as oxygen levels collapse is less questioned.

While much of the Australian public now find battery-hen farming anathema, the hyper-intensive nature of salmon farming and its environmental consequences are far from common knowledge. And as the idea of chickens as animals that experience suffering is only a few decades old, the idea that salmon suffer is so new that it generates no regulatory interest or public outrage.

Yet we know that salmon do suffer. Over the last twenty years substantial scientific evidence has emerged that demonstrates fish experience pain.[110] A 2016 Norwegian scientific study found that common industrial practices with salmon, such as 'stripping of broodstock [mature fish used for breeding], handling, vaccination, crowding, grading, starvation, anti-microbial treatments as well as loading and transport can lead to an increased susceptibility to a wide range of diseases. These stressors can also lead to injury and the impaired performance of reared salmon, which are usually kept in crowded conditions which facilitate the transmission of infectious pathologies.'[111]

For densely packed Tasmanian salmon feedlots, every summer brings with it multiple fatal plagues—low oxygen, gill disease, jellyfish blooms, pilchard virus—that the salmon survive only through a regime of invasive machine handling known as 'bathing', a misnomer suggesting something gentle for what is in reality a violent industrial process in which the salmon are treated as production units being cleansed; a practice at once stressful and dangerous for the fish, which results in numerous injuries and mortalities, and in some instances mass deaths. In 2018, a Tassal farm in Tasmania killed 30,000 fish during a 'bathing' treatment, citing 'human error' as the cause.[112]

A detailed 2016 Norwegian study published by the Royal Society found that industrially farmed salmon suffer sufficient stress and depression to deform and stunt their very growth. Stunted salmon are a common and costly feature of farming, affecting up to 25 per cent of fish.[113] This is strange in itself: growth-stunted sheep are not a common feature of sheep farming.

The Norwegian scientists pointed out that Atlantic salmon have gone through a rapid and intense domestication, which 'challenges individuals with a series of stressors that do not occur in nature'.[114] The scientists concluded, 'The behavioural and serotonergic profile exhibited by GS [growth-stunted] fish is reminiscent of a depressed state, similar to those described in mammals.'[115]

Trapped in an aquatic torture dome, many salmon respond as other sentient creatures do to torment, stress, noise, overcrowding, aggression and cannibalism: by simply not growing, or dying. Pictures of growth-stunted salmon—small, sad, deformed creatures—next to healthy salmon can be found in the scientific literature,[116] but are never seen in the promotion of salmon by governments, industry or its largest retailers, Coles and Woolworths. The losses of salmon consequent on these many problems are extraordinary, and larger fish kills—events where hundreds of thousands of salmon die—are unwelcome but far from unknown. Tasmanian salmon corporations routinely accept stock losses of 10 per cent. What sheep farmer would accept that level of loss?

Raising further questions about their welfare are the numerous deformities industrially produced salmon commonly have—from missing outer fins rubbed away from the circular swimming motion, grotesque underbite and overbites, through to spinal deformation. Research by Melbourne University scientists found that half of all farmed salmon suffer deafness, being bred with deformed ear bones. The deformity, rare in wild fish, begins in hatcheries, 'but its effects on hearing become increasingly more severe as the fish age'. Afflicted fish can lose up to 50 per cent of their hearing.[117]

If this wasn't bad enough, the Tasmanian salmon industry, almost alone in the world, goes so far as to chromosomally alter a proportion of its fish by a process that sees salmon eggs being subjected to what the RSPCA describes as 'thermal or pressure shocks' to create a sterile creature with three sets of chromosomes.[118]

The fish that results—known as a triploid—is prone to a range of health problems but is faster growing and fatter. It grows so quickly that it suffers a range of physical deformities, from oversized lower jaws (up to 30 per cent), to spinal problems so bad they affect swimming, to heart deformities, to cataracts and reduced gill surfaces. In consequence, there is also a much higher mortality among triploids.[119] These

Frankenfish are bred to suffer, but even after accounting for the higher mortality rates, the profit from them is high. So, in addition to the upwards of one in ten fish that will die before slaughter, the one in four that fails to grow properly because of stress and depression-like symptoms, up to one in three triploids may suffer difficulties in even moving—having been hormonally deformed to be that way.

Commenting on her 2016 report on industrial salmon health problems, Tormey Reimer, then of the University of Melbourne's School of BioSciences, said, 'Producing farmed animals with deformities contravenes two of the Five Freedoms that form the basis of legislation to ensure the welfare of farmed animals in many countries.'[120]

The Five Freedoms had their origins in a highly influential 1964 British book called *Animal Machines*. Horrified by the new factory farming and inspired by the example of Rachel Carson, whose *Silent Spring* had two years before exposed the evils of widespread chemical use in agriculture, the English Quaker Ruth Harrison wrote one of the first sustained critiques of the industrialisation of animal production.[121] The spotlight it threw on the cruelties of intensive poultry and livestock production led to a British parliamentary inquiry and legal reform. One of the inquiry's findings became the basis of the Five Freedoms—five rules of animal welfare.[122] In 1993, the RSPCA in Australia adopted the Five Freedoms as policy.[123]

And yet, in spite of salmon farming seeming to be in clear contravention of three of the Five Freedoms— the freedom from discomfort, the freedom to express normal behaviour and the freedom from fear and distress—the RSPCA endorses Huon Aquaculture under its Approved Farming Scheme. This endorsement is used widely in Huon's marketing of their salmon, from stickers prominently displayed on its products to its website.[124]

Between 2012 and 2018 the World Wildlife Foundation (WWF) also allowed Tassal to use its logo on its products as an assurance that its salmon was 'responsibly sourced'. According to ASX documents, in the 2016 financial year alone, Tassal paid WWF $250,000 for 'services and conservation projects'. The WWF endorsement of Tassal was used by criminologist Paul Bleakley in 2019 as an example 'of a corrupt corporate arrangement that is designed purposefully to mislead consumers'.[125]

When questioned about its endorsement, the RSPCA said Huon Aquaculture had to meet 'the RSPCA's detailed animal welfare standards . . . underpinned by the principles of the Five Freedoms'. When asked what they were paid for their endorsement of Huon Aquaculture's farmed salmon, the RSPCA declined to respond, citing confidentiality.

In 2020 it was revealed that the RSPCA in Britain had received £500,000 a year to endorse the Scottish farmed salmon industry, prompting Chris Packham, one of Britain's leading naturalists and an RSPCA (UK) vice-president, to tweet to his 386,000 followers, 'Open cage salmon farming is fraught with very serious issues and clearly needs reform/ regulation/ cessation. I will . . . work urgently towards a renewed position from their POV. I'm on it!'[126] Later that year, in a new book, Packham described salmon farming as 'a grim apocalypse fuelled by power and profits'.[127]

The RSPCA policy dealing with its endorsement of Huon Aquaculture could not be clearer. It unambiguously states that 'the triploidisation process and the farming of triploid salmon are not permitted' as well as 'the farming of salmon in Macquarie Harbour, Tasmania is not permitted'.[128] And yet Huon continues to grow triploid salmon in Macquarie Harbour, 'to ensure continuous supply of the desired fish size to the market all year round', though, depending on its audience, it claims to be growing different numbers of fish there.[129]

On its website, aimed at consumers, Huon says, 'The RSPCA's standard for farmed Atlantic salmon does not allow for the farming of salmon in Macquarie Harbour therefore, 98 per cent of Huon's salmon is currently farmed to the standard',[130] a figure also quoted by the RSPCA in response to inquiries made in March 2021. Yet in its 2020 annual report, aimed at investors and the higher standards demanded by fiscal regulatory authorities, Huon Aquaculture says, 'less than 10% of Huon's salmon production comes from Macquarie Harbour'.[131]

The cost of keeping so many salmon alive in circumstances in which they would otherwise be dead is the destruction of the surrounding marine ecosystem, which over time transforms from a rich, healthy world of diverse and unique species into a sick monoculture, many parts of which are threatened and dying. Nothing better exemplifies the worsening environmental destruction loops into which salmon farming is locking some of Tasmania's most iconic coastal seascapes than jellyfish.

Jellyfish are a major problem for the salmon industry. Jellyfish kill salmon in hundreds of thousands by stinging them, suffocating them with mucus and damaging their gills. In years when jellyfish blooms are bad, the damage can be catastrophic: in 2019 Huon Aquaculture's annual profit was cut by 64 per cent because of jellyfish.[132] Yet the equation is brutally simple: more salmon equals more jellyfish. And more jellyfish beget more jellyfish.

Dr Lisa-ann Gershwin is a leading jellyfish expert who has written an acclaimed book on the subject.[133] Her research on the relationship between jellyfish and Tasmanian salmon farming makes nightmarish reading. For one more dirty secret of Tasmanian salmon farming is that it helps to create and drive the jellyfish blooms, and the proliferating jellyfish in turn drive the destruction of the marine ecosystem.

According to Dr Gershwin they do this in three ways.

First, jellyfish prefer artificial surfaces, making the ever-growing number of salmon cages 'an ideal habitat for jellyfish to flourish in'.[134] Salmon nets are perfect jellyfish nurseries.

Second, because of the threat jellyfish pose to salmon, salmon-feeding-lot nets are routinely cleaned using water blasting or brushing or scraping. And yet the very act of removing jellyfish multiplies them. Each resulting tiny fragment of broken jellyfish acts as a seed for a new colony, resulting in thousands more creatures than were washed off, while the remnants left on nets also remain capable of seeding more jellyfish.

'Hydroid seeding can be compared to the broom scene in the Disney film *Fantasia*,' writes Dr Gershwin, 'where each effort to destroy the brooms simply resulted in more brooms. Downstream hydroid seeding is a serious issue affecting farmed and native species alike. In the short term, it leads to a higher biomass of medusae stinging the salmon and native species, and in the long term, the extra biomass permanently alters the function of the ecosystem.'[135]

Third, the huge nutrient stream from salmon excrement acts as fertiliser, stimulating the growth of zooplankton, a primary food source for jellyfish. In this way, the exploding number of jellyfish (created by salmon farmers seeking to deal with the problem) find, in the zooplankton (also created by salmon farming), a perfect food to sustain a large jellyfish population. More nutrients in a marine ecosystem mean more zooplankton mean more jellyfish—and every six hours salmon farming pours another tonne of liquid fertiliser into D'Entrecasteaux Channel alone.

If jellyfish are a problem for corporate profits, they are a disaster for the environment. Jellyfish blooms are not only a key indicator of a marine ecosystem wildly out of balance. Established in sufficient scale, they can also drive an ecosystem so far out of balance that it may never recover, irretrievably destroying the environment.

'There is no question that [Tasmanian] salmon farming is affecting native species,' writes Dr Gershwin. 'The unresearched questions are how badly and how permanently.'[136]

As well as killing native fish species, jellyfish also adversely affect shellfish such as oysters, scallops, mussels and clams, along with sponges and polyps. Jellyfish have a huge appetite. The biggest impact the blooms have is on native fish, eating their eggs and larvae, as well as the plankton larvae that the surviving native fish would otherwise eat. When the jellyfish die off, they simply add to the nutrient load, creating a further positive feedback loop, producing yet more jellyfish.

The cumulative effect is to 'flip' an ecosystem to one in which jellyfish become dominant. Dr Gershwin regards this as 'unsustainable to both the long-term viability of this industry and to the environment in the broader sense'.[137]

The profound and perverse environmental imbalance created in Tasmania by industrial salmon production, the ways in which ecosystems are flipped to their detriment by salmon farming, are no better exemplified than by the example of long-nosed fur seals. Hunted to the point of near extinction in the nineteenth century, classified as a rare, threatened species in Tasmania and protected under state and federal law, the fur seals' fate at the hands of salmon farmers is particularly cruel.[138] While in South Australia fines of up to $100,000 can be imposed for killing a long-nosed fur seal, in Tasmania what is termed the 'management' of fur seals by salmon companies long ago crossed over into programs of systematic cruelty.

Seals represent one more insoluble problem for the salmon industry as they damage nets (and get trapped inside them), kill salmon, and interfere with divers. Yet offering a permanent food source, the floating feedlots that proliferate along the south-east Tasmanian coast are attracting fur seals in ever-growing numbers—in areas where they have not been known in living memory. The industry's war against the seals is never-ending: all that changes are the weapons used as one scandal begets another.

When the salmon farmers were found out to be shooting and killing seals on a large scale, dumping their rotting bodies on local tips,[139] the industry resorted to trapping and relocating the animals to north-west Tasmania. By 2017 over two thousand seals a year were being trapped, sedated and transported for several hours. There, the creatures established colonies that in turn became a major problem for local commercial fishermen. One, Craig Garland, in a submission to the Fin Fish Inquiry run by the Tasmanian government in 2019, claimed that the seals were rendering the fisheries of the north-west small-mesh fishermen uneconomical and 'resulting in mental health issues for those fishermen'.[140] The practice so incensed Garland that he ran for federal parliament on an anti-salmon industry platform in the critical 2018 Braddon by-election. In spite of spending no money on his campaign Garland still garnered 11 per cent of the vote, his preferences delivering the seat to the ALP candidate in what had been expected to be a Liberal Party victory.

As always with the salmon industry, many details of the trapping program are secret. A recent Right

to Information request by Environment Tasmania
revealed that in 2016 Tassal came under criminal investigation for animal cruelty after wildlife rangers found
twenty seals in a pen at a Tassal lease and it was subsequently discovered the seals might have been there
for several days without food or haul-out space.

Yet instead of pursuing prosecution, the Tasmanian
government quickly acted to cover up the scandal.
Tassal was retrospectively granted an extension to the
time it could keep the twenty seals captive—from six
hours to seven days. All charges were dropped and a
Marine Farming Branch bureaucrat advised Tassal on
how to spin the story to the media, should it become
public.[141]

In recent years the salmon industry has hit upon
seal deterrents more suggestive of suppressing a civil
uprising than responsible environmental management.
One of its method is to fire 'blunt darts' at the animals,
another is to shoot them with what the international
industry trade publication *Salmon Business* identified
as riot guns, using beanbag rounds—a cloth sock
enclosing 40 grams of lead pellets fired from 12-gauge
shotguns.[142] According to Right to Information documents, in 2016 alone 3770 beanbag rounds were used.[143]
Though described as non-lethal, such ammunition
has been associated with deaths and severe injuries to
humans in the US, Hong Kong and Europe.[144] As well as

poisoning the marine environment with 150 kilograms of lead every year, in 2018, according to an ABC report, 'two industry insiders who work in aquaculture in Tasmania . . . independently claimed that on a number of occasions they had personally witnessed beanbag rounds blinding seals and hitting them in the head at close range'.[145]

In the view of Malcolm Caulfield, founder and principal lawyer of the Animal Welfare Community Legal Centre Tasmania, 'What we are seeing is an industrial-scale use of cruel measures against a protected species in Tasmanian waters.

'What it clearly highlights to me is that the Government isn't doing its job. The fact of the matter is this is an unacceptable use of these very violent tactics against these marine mammals which have a high level of protected status under the law.'[146]

All of this is ignored by Tasmanian politicians and regulators. The war simply goes on. The state government—which once paid Tasmanians to hunt the thylacine to extinction—continues to permit the trapping and sedation of seals, while allowing their killing as 'a management option of last resort'.[147] Tassal is reportedly now trialling a new deterrent, again borrowed from riot control, that of water cannons, which it describes as spraying seals with a 'low-pressure, high flow' water stream.

'This is still a noxious deterrent that has potential to injure seals,' the RSPCA's chief executive Dr Andrew Byrne has been quoted as saying. 'The RSPCA would prefer investigating options that may encourage the seals to move away from pens or the holy grail of seal safety, better pen designs.'[148]

Like so many unfixed, unresolved and ultimately unresolvable problems with salmon farming, the Tasmanian salmon industry has been talking about seal-proofing nets for almost as long as there has been a Tasmanian salmon industry. The companies do invest significantly in improving their net technology because loss of stock represents loss of profit, but a failsafe design remains elusive and the war between Big Salmon and the marine environment continues to escalate.

In that war, the most common weapon used against seals is the innocuously named 'seal cracker'. In the US it is more accurately called a seal bomb and is classified as a 'high explosive' by the U.S. Bureau of Alcohol, Tobacco, Firearms, and Explosives. Either lit and thrown into the water, or set up as booby-trapped underwater devices, seal bombs 'have been shown to shatter bones of marine mammals and to kill fish within the blast vicinity'.[149] In one instance, a seal bomb killed a human swimmer. The victim was found to have 'ruptured both eardrums, herniated brain tissue through ruptured areas in the cribriform plates, fractured cranial bones including the wings of the sphenoid and the left petrosal, and caused a 1.5-cm-deep wound above the scapula'.[150]

In 2016 the Tasmanian salmon industry used *39,024* seal bombs, and yet no research has been conducted on their actual physical impact on fur seals, nor is there any consideration given or science being undertaken on their consequences on the surrounding marine environment, though it may be grave.[151] Dead seals are often found washed up near Tasmanian salmon farms.

Off the southern tip of Bruny Island, the only part of Bruny now not afflicted by the ever-growing blight of the salmon industry's floating feedlots, Rob Pennicott's celebrated boat tours—a centrepiece of Tasmanian tourism—showcase dolphins and southern right and humpback whales to delighted tourists. A genuine conservationist, Pennicott's iconic business is marketed with an image that captures the spirit of Bruny Island: a dolphin cavorting. But elsewhere on the island—one of Tasmania's tourist hotspots—its waterways, particularly D'Entrecasteaux Channel, are being transformed into heavy industrial sites where native animals are blinded and wounded as a matter of routine management, and dolphins, not so long ago common, are now rarely sighted.

According to Gerard Castles, vice-president of the Friends of North Bruny, dolphins have largely vanished in the northern reaches of D'Entrecasteaux Channel in recent years, and locals believe it is because of the salmon industry's use of underwater explosive devices. They now also worry about the effect of seal bombs on whales.

It has long been known that whales and dolphins rely on sound for everything from communication to foraging to navigation, mating and parental bonding. Conversely, ocean noise pollution has been recognised for decades as a threat to marine mammals, which can lead to behavioural changes such as altered migration and foraging patterns.[152]

In Scotland, underwater transducers—known as acoustic deterrent devices (ADDs)—that 'use sound pressure at a specific frequency to cause discomfort to seals' are commonly deployed on salmon farms as a deterrent.[153] A leaked memo from the Head of Policy and Advice at Scottish Natural Heritage in 2017 found 'sufficient evidence, both empirical and modelled, to show that ADDs can cause disturbance and displacement of cetaceans'. The memo went on to state, 'There is sound, scientific evidence to expect that hearing damage, stress and masking may also occur.'[154]

Seal bombs are a low-tech version of an ADD, but a far more brutal one. Exploding seal bombs produce intense waterborne pressure waves of impulsive and broadband noise, which can affect cetaceans up to

118 kilometres away from the blast.[155] Precisely because dolphins and whales are affected by these bombs, their use was banned as early as 1990 in the US's Pacific tuna fishery.[156] A recent American study on the effect of such bombs used to disperse sea lions showed the explosions adversely affected Monterey porpoises, damaging their hearing and interfering with essential activities such as feeding and reproduction, tens of kilometres from the blast site.[157]

Adding to the grotesque sonic hell around salmon farming zones, where tens of thousands of times a year marine animals are pummelled by violent underwater pressure waves created by seal bombs—pressure waves so intense that they can force scuba divers out of the water[158]—is the incessant and growing cacophony of heavy industrial noise from the ever-larger boats and giant factory ships deployed by the salmon industry. These are some of the biggest commercial boats operating in Tasmania, including the largest well boat in the world, and they relentlessly thud their way up and down narrow, shallow inshore waterways.

Shipping noise is increasingly recognised as a significant source of underwater noise pollution that adversely affects aquatic animals, and it has become a major concern for regulators around the world in terms of cetacean conservation.[159] Research undertaken by Curtin University's Centre for Marine Science and Technology shows shipping noise is 'especially worrying for baleen whales, including right whales which specialise in low frequency calls . . . in certain circumstances, noise can also affect the vestibular system, reproductive system, nervous system and other tissues and organs of marine animals.'[160] According to a Victorian Department of Sustainability and Environment report, southern right whales 'are extremely sensitive to sounds below and above the water surface [and] . . . human activities which produce loud and persistent sounds under water may interfere with whale activity and induce significant levels of stress. This could cause changes in use of specific habitat areas by the whales.'[161] A 2016 British study on humpback whales in North Atlantic coastal waters found that shipping noise 'could potentially lead to population-level impacts'.[162]

Between May and December humpback and southern right whales are sighted regularly on Tasmania's east coast as they migrate northwards. In recent years a number of juvenile humpbacks have remained in the Derwent and Storm Bay area for several months. Some southern right whales give birth in Tasmanian waters. Yet, according to Gerard Castles, they are sighted much less frequently now in the most industrialised waterway, D'Entrecasteaux Channel, and he says locals are fearful of how the increasing industrialisation of Storm Bay, with its huge salmon farms, will ultimately impact on whale numbers there. Fears are also held for the Tasmanian east coast more generally, should salmon farmers succeed in a sea grab there.

Perversely, white pointer sharks are attracted by low-frequency industrial noise, according to Chris Black, Tasmania's leading authority on these sharks. As seals are drawn to floating feedlots because they are sources of salmon, seals in turn attract large sharks, particularly white pointers, into waterways that are among the most popular in Tasmania with swimmers, divers, tourists and recreational boaters. Industrial noise is like a dinner bell for a naturally inquisitive, intelligent creature like a great white, according to Black, serving as a sonic attraction that alerts them to the presence of seals.

For fish farmers, the white pointers are welcome as a natural predator of seals. In his work on these sharks in Tasmania, Black quotes a manager of the Tassal fish farm at Nubeena saying of a great white lurking around his salmon farm: 'There's a slight worry from a human point of view, but I'm absolutely ecstatic that's he's eating seals . . . I'd put him on the payroll . . . If I could have one set up shop here all the time, I'd be a pretty happy farm manager, I've got to say.'[163] Those who surf at popular Roaring Beach only a few kilometres away, who swim the nearby beaches, and who dive for scallops and crayfish in nearby areas, may beg to differ.

No science has been commissioned by the Tasmanian salmon industry or the state government to examine the effects of salmon farming's incessant use of explosives on the whale and dolphin population, nor what effect the ever-increasing noise of the farms—giant factory ships and the heavy industrial paraphernalia that cover every farm—is having on these marine mammals.

At Hobart Airport, visitors are still greeted at the baggage carousel by a seal statue circulating on the luggage belt advertising boat tours around Bruny Island's south coast.

'A more accurate image for Bruny Island', says Gerard Castles, 'would be a dead or dying seal, with shotgun or seal bomb injuries.'

For the tourists on those boat trips along Bruny Island's southern end, where salmon farms and their attendant big ships have not yet reached nor yet their collateral destruction touched, the sight and sound of the dolphins and whales—once a perennial element of the island's magical allure—can still be experienced. But for many Bruny Islanders, particularly those on the Channel, such wonders are rapidly becoming one more sad memory. The former playground where the creatures' broaching forms ploughed the light is now a darkening spiderweb of giant nets, seal bomb explosions, throbbing diesels and huge factory ships, around which drift the spectre of ever-growing jellyfish blooms.

5

INVENTED IN THE FAR COLDER, MUCH DEEPER fjords of Norway, salmon farming seemed at first even better suited to the shallow inshore waterways of Tasmania. Nowhere else in the world were salmon grown in such warm waters and, in consequence, nowhere else could they be grown so quickly, the Tasmanian fish maturing within eighteen months, a year quicker than anywhere else.[164] But as the CSIRO put it in 2020, this faster growth came 'at a cost'.[165] And that cost was to be paid by the environment and the Tasmanian people.

From the beginning, Atlantic salmon were the wrong species in the wrong environment. Unlike the brown and rainbow trout, which were successfully introduced to Tasmanian waters, and despite repeated attempts in Tasmania from 1865 to the 1930s, no self-perpetuating population of Atlantic salmon in the wild was ever established.[166] Salmon grow best in seawaters of between 12 and 15°C. Above 17°C the fish become so badly stressed that, according to a Huon Aquaculture discussion paper, 'growth and development is impaired'.[167] Summer coastal water temperatures in Tasmania can average more than 19°C for several weeks.[168] Even in 1985 the waters were too hot for growing salmon.

Warmer waters coupled with overstocking led to low oxygen levels that could cause mass fish kills at summer's height. In the early days, the Tasmanian industry responded to these fish kills by installing heavy diesel compressors on their farms, which blew bubbles up through the nets, oxygenating the water, a 24/7 process known as 'venturation', and the beginning of the increasing industrialisation of the island's serene waterways.

But a worse problem became apparent almost from the beginning. Previously unknown mass outbreaks of gill amoeba (*Neoparamoeba pemaquidensis*)—a microscopic organism endemic to southern Tasmanian waters that attaches to fish gills, clogging them and preventing the flow of oxygen—began occurring in salmon pens each summer. Left untended, amoebic gill disease killed up to 50 per cent of salmon stock.[169]

A solution was found by towing giant bladders containing tonnes of freshwater sourced from all over Tasmania's dry south-east—public and private water systems, reservoirs and dams—to the floating feedlots ringworming their way around Bruny Island and up the Huon River. Millions of salmon would be mechanically vacuumed from their nets into the bladders, flushed there in a soup of freshwater that killed the saltwater amoeba, vacuumed up again and pumped back into their saltwater pens. Afterwards, the polluted freshwater would be dumped into the marine environment used as commercial and recreational fisheries. Though there was little benign about such a violent process, its pollution or its growing massive water footprint, the industry gave it a benign misnomer: fish bathing.

To begin with, fish bathing occurred only once or twice a season. But when the seas stayed warm, fish were soon reinfected. Bathing became a monthly and sometimes even fortnightly event and, as the summer season extended, bathing could be repeated for upwards of half the year.[170] What was once occasional became essential, and what at first had had little impact became a series of related problems—an escalating freshwater footprint, marine pollution and noise—none of which regulators addressed. All that mattered to government was that it enabled the industry to survive and prosper, whatever the warnings and consequences.

Unknown in 1985 was that the Tasmanian salmon industry was trying to grow a cold-water species in one of the fastest-heating seas in the world. By the

2000s the industry was aware that climate change was 'both a current and a long-term challenge' that led to 'degraded fish health, increased disease outbreaks and mortality'.[171]

While Tasmania's giant kelp forests—the nursery of its unique coastal marine ecology—have almost all vanished from its east-coast waters, and its cold-water fish species are declining, in recent years more than *sixty* species of fish from subtropical waters have established populations in Tasmanian waters, and coral reefs are forming in Bass Strait. By 2020 the seas off Tasmania's east coast had transformed into a global hotspot for climate change, having already risen by almost 2°C, heating nearly four times faster than the global average, and expected to heat a further 2 to 3 degrees by 2070.

Amid such epochal change, Tasmania's south-east coast—which even in 1985 had been on the very edge of viability for salmon survival but had looked so promising for industrial production of the fish—could now only be sustained through an ever-increasing mix of antibiotic use and bathing.

Within twenty years, fish bathing—and its massive diesel bill—represented 20 per cent of the total production cost of Tasmanian salmon. In consequence, the carbon emissions of Tasmanian salmon farms were found in a 2013 study to be extraordinarily high. Every tonne of Tasmanian salmon emitted 506 kilograms of CO_2-e on the marine-farm side of its production alone—almost ten times that of the Norwegian industry (whose emissions were at 46.2 kg CO_2-e), which was the lowest of salmon producers, and five times that of Chile (100 kg CO_2-e), the worst of all other global producers.[172]

As the sea warmed, the salmon corporations' thirst for freshwater grew enormous. The secrecy with which the industry cloaks itself makes it impossible to determine its exact amount of freshwater use. But the available evidence suggests it's huge. According to an industry-sanctioned study in 2013, producing one tonne of gutted Tasmanian salmon requires 66 tonnes (kilo-litres) of freshwater, 90 per cent of which is consumed by fish bathing, with most of the rest used for hatcheries.[173]

In 2013–14, Tasmania produced approximately 41,000 tonnes of salmon, of which approximately 8000 tonnes were produced in Macquarie Harbour, where fish bathing isn't regularly used. Using the 2013 study's figures, that would mean at least 1.96 million tonnes of freshwater were drawn down, polluted and dumped back into rich marine ecosystems.

Although the salmon companies publicly claim to have reduced their freshwater usage in recent years, their own figures suggest that it is a growing problem. By 2020 Tassal alone, on its own figures, would appear to be using more than 2 million tonnes of freshwater for bathing.[174]

But the total numbers are unknown and effectively unknowable. There is no comprehensive public register of how much freshwater is used. While the EPA can only advise that 'industry is likely best placed to respond to the quantity of freshwater utilised for bathing', the figures released by salmon companies are partial and appear contradictory. Huon Aquaculture, for example, in their 2019 submission to the Legislative Council Inquiry into Fin Fish Farming, claimed its total use of all freshwater in 2019 was 1100 megalitres (this included use of Huon-owned dam water and river-mouth water) while their usage of town-supplied water for bathing (not including dam or river water use) was 1699 mega-litres. No explanation of these seemingly conflicting figures was offered.[175]

Freshwater bathing is entirely unregulated, leaving salmon companies free to dump the immense amounts of used, polluted water wherever and however they want, without informing the public. On top of the secrecy is a convenient ignorance. The effects of dumping massive and growing amounts of polluted freshwater remain unknown, unmeasured and unreported.

To lower the diesel, labour and maintenance costs of freshwater fish bathing, both Tassal and Huon have in the last few years introduced gigantic factory ships, known as well boats. At 112 metres long, with a carrying capacity of 12,450 tonnes of water, Huon Aquaculture's

Ronja Storm was at the time of its commissioning the largest well boat in the world, twice the size of any other on the planet. The giant factory ships have a variety of uses but are primarily for fish bathing. They operate around the clock, with crews living on board, entirely outside of EPA regulations.

They also feature desalination plants to which no environmental regulations apply. The salmon companies claim their plants will reduce freshwater use, though, anecdotally, the companies prefer not to source their water from desalination unless necessary, as it is far cheaper to use terrestrial freshwater. But when the desalination plants are used, where and how is the highly concentrated, toxic saline released?

In spite of Tasmania's reputation as a wet state, heavy rainfall is a feature of the island's west but not its dry eastern half, parts of which have recorded rainfalls in recent years as low as that of Bourke in outback New South Wales.[176] South-east Tasmania is frequently water-stressed, Hobart being the second-driest capital in Australia after Adelaide. If the industry is to double in size by 2030, as it intends, within fewer than ten years it could be using well over six million tonnes of freshwater just for bathing—and from where is that freshwater to come?

There are so many questions raised by fish bathing not even unanswered but unasked. Why no public records? Why no reporting? Why no studies? And the most obvious of all: why no regulations?

The government not only has no idea how much freshwater the salmon industry uses at present, it also has no idea from where, in the future, a doubling in supply of freshwater for the industry is to come. Nor has it examined how the further depletion of already limited freshwater stocks will affect other users.

We do know that any future planning for the salmon industry will *not* factor in its impacts on local freshwater supply and the knock-on effects to other industries and communities. And we do know what happens when a community comes between a salmon farm and freshwater.

The community loses.

In 2017 Tassal opened a controversial fish farm on Tasmania's east coast at Okehampton Bay, in the face of major community opposition. According to a person with knowledge of the contract, who spoke on the condition of anonymity, Tassal sought the Glamorgan Spring Bay Council's approval to build for Okehampton a water supply system including a dam, principally for fish bathing at their Okehampton farm, for which Tassal would pay. But in a meeting with Tassal, the former mayor, the late Michael Kent, not only endorsed the project but mysteriously agreed that his council would pay for it in its entirety.

The contract Glamorgan Spring Bay Council then signed was wholly disadvantageous to the council and ruinous to its ratepayers. The only beneficiary of the deal was Tassal, even though it didn't pay a cent for the scheme's construction and would pay for water only retrospectively, every twelve months. While the scheme was publicly lauded as making water available to other users—meaning farmers—contractually this could only happen with Tassal's prior permission, a detail never publicly admitted. The project ended up blowing out in cost to approximately $9 million. The Glamorgan Spring Bay Council, which has only five thousand ratepayers and at the time an annual budget of less than $10 million, ran out of money to complete the water scheme.

Teetering on bankruptcy, the council asked Tassal if it would foot the final $600,000 the council needed to finish the scheme, which would exist solely for Tassal's benefit. Tassal refused, pointing out that the council was contractually bound to build the scheme. Further loans were taken out by the council and local rates were put up to cover the cost.

The Okehampton farm, which Tassal claimed would employ a hundred locals, today employs around twenty full-time workers. By way of comparison, the nearby eco-tourism resort Spring Bay Mill—set up by Wotif.com founder Graeme Wood on the site of what was once the world's biggest wood-chip mill as an example of an alternative economic model to Tasmania's resource industries—employs 35 full-time workers. Since it commenced operations at Okehampton, Tassal has used the drinking water supply of Orford—the principal town in Tasmania's driest municipality—for its farm, and is now also contractually entitled to use the council-provided raw water pipeline, taken from the same dam. When Tassal boasts in its marketing materials of 'Our Communities', it's saying no more than the truth: it owns communities, and in Tassal's eyes they owe the company, a relationship more feudal than fair and respectful.

Fish bathing robs communities of their ever-scarcer freshwater resources, while charging councils for them. As one local put it, it's like getting the bill for the getaway car after your house has been burgled. Fish bathing also increases salmon farmers' carbon footprint to a point where any claims of environmental credentials smack of hypocrisy. It pollutes the marine environment in ways that are little understood and entirely unregulated.

And fish bathing is noisy.

This noise is one more element of the pollution from salmon farms that was well enough known as a problem over a quarter of a century ago for the

Productivity Commission in its 1996 report to observe that Tasmanian salmon farming 'may have adverse effects on nearby property values, because [fish] farm structures, excessive noise and the glare of lights may result in a loss of amenity to residential properties on adjacent foreshores.'[177] But nothing was done.

Over the next quarter of a century, instead of working to rectify the problem, regulators allowed it to steadily deteriorate. Rather than standards being slowly raised, the very opposite happened. Every year in previously tranquil coastal communities throughout south-east Tasmania, noise pollution from salmon farms grows worse, more widespread and more unaccountable.

From Long Bay at Port Arthur, where Tassal offered $50 salmon vouchers to those who suffered noise, to Nubeena and White Beach on the west Tasman Peninsula, to Dennes Point and Killora on North Bruny, to Conleys Beach on South Bruny, to Tinderbox and Middleton on the far side of the Channel, to the lower Huon, to Port Huon, locals have been subjected to daily and nightly barrages of noise: low droning and constant heavy industrial noise from barge drops, cranes, venturation generators, feed compressors and net-washing machines.

In addition to floodlights shining into bedrooms all night and the growing cacophony arising from the heavy industrialisation of the floating feedlot system, locals suffer the noise of an armada of salmon boats, from small runabouts to giant ships, which service the farms round the clock, sometimes only hundreds of metres from people's homes. The thudding diesels of tugs, trawlers, barges, service vessels, harvest ships and, in the last few years, the gigantic well boats that serve to transport, bathe and grade fish, all now subject communities to noise pollution louder than ever before.

Salmon companies taunt locals when they complain, telling them and local media they are fully compliant with regulations. This is a cruel joke at locals' expense, given the companies know full well that despite decades of complaints, most fish farms to this day have *no noise regulations* attached to their environmental lease conditions because government refuses to recognise the noise as a problem. The EPA has general noise limit guidelines but these, conveniently for the salmon industry, are unenforcable by the EPA.[178] Because Tasmanian regulators refuse to recognise the many ships and boats that form the mechanical, industrial and logistical hub of industrial salmon production as fundamental to the industry, no noise regulations beyond those existing under marine law apply. The vessels are allowed to ply the often narrow coastal inshore waterways day and night, no matter that the marine law was never meant to apply to factories operating next door to people's homes.

But in Tasmania, when it comes to salmon farms, the salmon farms are the law.

Dr Maureen Ryan of Cygnet—a town on the Huon River, along the lower reaches of which the salmon industry's floating feedlots now proliferate—is seeing increasing numbers of patients presenting with depression and stress-related illness attributable to noise pollution from salmon farming. Some sell up, some give up, some have their lives destroyed. Witness after witness from coastal communities testified to the 2019 Tasmanian parliamentary inquiry into salmon farming about the ways their lives were being affected by the farms' noise pollution.

'The low-frequency drone of the engines and hydraulic equipment that can go on for hours is very distressing,' testified Melinda Huck of Gunpowder Jetty, North West Bay. 'It can be heard through our double-glazed windows and has on occasions caused the windows to rattle and pictures on the wall to shake . . . We feel very strongly that it is not appropriate for what is effectively heavy industrial activity to be carried out close to a residential area. It is disruptive and distressing . . . My husband works in mining and is incredulous about the level of impact that these operations can get away with.'[179]

'The noise is like having a revving tractor on your front lawn. It is impossible to sleep without earplugs and white noise,' according to Tony Mahood of Middleton in the Channel. 'Surely we all have the right to live in a peaceful and quiet environment in our homes. Or at least the right to a peaceful night's sleep.'[180]

Sharon Moore of the lower Channel is 'kept awake for hours at night and woken in the very early hours by the noise from the Huon Aquaculture well boats . . . I know of people who live much closer to the route; their lives would be a misery . . . I have heard of the enormous amount of stress, with ensuing health problems, suffered by people who have tried to enter the labyrinthine bureaucracy involved in trying to deal with noise and light problems from fish-farming operations. It seems that there is nothing but buck-passing and mis- or inadequate information.'[181]

And so it goes on—and on and on, night after night, year after year, decade after decade, with neither government nor industry taking any responsibility for the excessive noise pollution and the human damage it causes.

One story must suffice for many.

Miranda Howie is an artist who many years ago, when she found a property on a gravel road that tracked alongside a eucalypt-lined stretch of the Huon River's estuary, thought she had come upon one of the most beautiful places on Earth. 'I was so happy,' she says when I meet with her.

And then a small salmon farm less than three hundred metres from her home began to grow. The number of attendant boats grew with it—the speed boats with workers going back and forth all day, the feed boats, the net washers, the factory boats collecting and grading fish, the boats delivering fish, the boats moving nets, the tugs and ancient trawlers dragging nets and water bladders. The compressors started up— the venturation compressors to aerate the low oxygen water through summers that each year grew a little longer; the feed compressors: on and on—all diesel machinery, more and more diesel machinery. Other salmon farms began appearing nearby. If the farm next to Miranda sometimes quietened down, others filled the void with their noise.

She went to the Marine Farming Branch. A noise logger was installed and discovered that when all the farm machinery was switched off, the silence was so intense that it fell below the capacity of the logger to record it.

The Marine Farming Branch officers did nothing.

Miranda discovered that she had no rights. If an industrial factory had been opened next door, she would have had rights and protections, but when the industrial factory was a salmon farm, no industrial regulations seemed to apply. Because the farm was on the water, council rules and regulations didn't apply.

Because the boats were not a fixed part of the salmon farm's industrial infrastructure, no noise rules applied. And the rules that did apply to the farm were so ludicrously loose as to be meaningless.

In her powerlessness, Miranda was reduced to making complaints to a salmon company that cared only about profit. Fish farm workers would rev boats outside her house just, she believes, to bully and intimidate. Day and night the noise would continue, the occasional breaks into silence becoming for Miranda the cruellest of all torments as she waited anxiously for the moment when the noise would restart. More boats came; larger, noisier boats, shuddering her home.

'It is only one small thing,' she says, 'when you think of everything else they have done. The Huon was chockers with fish when I came. Now you couldn't catch a cold down there.' She produces a box of plastic rubbish picked up on the foreshore below her house— black plastic shavings, clips, pipes, ropes, netting—so much plastic from the fish farm. Thick mats of algae blasted off the nets. She laughs about the things the salmon companies have got away with—the tonnes of copper formerly used as anti-fouling on their nets, all washed into the once glorious, now heavy-metal-contaminated Huon waters.

'Sound is an energy,' Miranda says. 'It hits you. It squeezes your heart.' She begins to cry. 'Diesels are not a rhythm,' she says. 'They're an uneven thing. I began getting headaches. I got sick. I can't get better.' She couldn't work at her art any longer. She couldn't look after her garden or her house. Things that had been a joy were now a torment. 'I can't swim down there, knowing what's in the water.' She shows me oyster shells. Some are gentle objects, an off-white, like cream calcified, thick and smooth to hold. 'That's before the farm,' she says. Others are a green-grey, a dystopian colour, and where the white oyster shells are whole, these are strangely brittle, ridden with cavities like rotten teeth. These are the only oyster shells she finds now. 'They're sick, too,' she says. 'Look at them.'

Her headaches rarely leave her. She has what she calls 'a heart thing'. One day she felt a vein in her forehead pulsing weirdly as her headache grew worse. She put her finger to it and felt the same cruel throb in her blood as in the woof-woof of the diesels. She cries again. So it has gone for fifteen years. She has lost friends, grown old, and fears she is lost. But she promised the trees on the riverbank, the eucalypts that stood sentinel over the river when she first found her home, and which so enchanted her when she first drove down that dusty road. She promised them she would not give up.

'Noise is an injustice,' Miranda says. 'But it's only one small thing.' Her table is covered with documents, which I now realise are her collected records of her fifteen years of living next to a salmon farm. There are official reports, legislation, articles, letters, the scattered detritus of a life trying to find some key that might open the door to some justice, some right as a citizen to not have her life ruined by the greed of a corporation; and not one document had opened one door.

The use of noise in interrogation and torture is well documented. Noise does not have to be loud, only sustained, to break its intended victim. A 2004 US program memo on CIA interrogation techniques notes how, at its now notorious Black Sites, 'the HVD [high value detainee] will be exposed to white noise/ loud sounds (not to exceed 79 decibels) and constant light during portions of the interrogation process'. In this way 'the HVD is typically reduced to a baseline, dependent state ... Establishing this baseline state is important to demonstrate to the HVD that he has no control over basic human needs.'[182]

Later that day I meet a young woman whose life was so broken by fish-farm noise, by that *one small thing*, that last year she attempted suicide.

A heart thing.

The CIA memo could be describing the way in which Miranda's and the young woman's lives were destroyed. Individuals, betrayed by a government that acts solely for the salmon companies, are left with only the salmon companies to directly deal with. Noise has become a form of control by salmon companies over communities whose sole way of addressing the basic human need for tranquillity is by begging the company's indulgence. The salmon farmers' so-called 'community liaison officers' engage in an elaborate theatre, the only purpose of which is to divide and deceive community members with untruths, promises that are not honoured and commitments that are routinely broken, but never to seriously deal with the problems of noise and light pollution that only worsen with every passing year.

When the young woman spoke out publicly about the noise pollution at a public meeting, dead wallabies with cut throats appeared in her front garden. A few months after our interview I email her seeking permission to publish her story. She replies with a thoughtful note, giving her permission but asking that her name not be used as she fears for herself and her family if she were to be identified.

Some will say such fear is not founded in reality, others that it sadly is. I met it enough times in the course of researching this book to know that it is genuinely held. As the salmon farm employees who revved their boats outside Miranda Howie's home understood: noise is power.

Tassal has it. Huon Aquaculture has it. Petuna has it. Tasmanians do not.

6

ROWAN ARMITAGE ACQUIRED THE MARINE farming lease to Okehampton Bay on Tasmania's east coast in the early 2000s, planning to farm salmon there. He spent $25,000 on a baseline scientific survey, which found the site was too shallow, lacking sufficient tidal and current flush to clear away fish faeces, and the waters too warm to sustain intensive salmon farming without substantial fish kills and damage to the marine environment.

In 2007 Armitage sold the lease to Spring Bay Seafoods. They used it to farm mussels, but when the site proved too warm even for the hardy shellfish, which died en masse, Spring Bay Seafoods rented the lease to Tassal.

Armitage was shocked to discover that Tassal planned to use the Okehampton site for salmon. He spoke out publicly against the proposed farm. When Tassal discovered Armitage still had the baseline scientific data demonstrating the site's unsuitability, he says he received a phone call from Tassal asking to buy his data. He refused. He began receiving anonymous calls from a blocked number offering him ever-larger sums for the data. Each time he refused, the price went up, until it peaked at $500,000. Armitage believed the calls were from Tassal and that they wanted the data in order to bury it.

'Why else was it worth so much?' he asks.

Not long after Armitage's final refusal to sell, there was a series of fresh anonymous phone calls, again from a blocked number, in which threats were made that he would be bankrupted, his credibility attacked and his character destroyed.

As Armitage tells me this story in a Hobart cafe, he becomes visibly shaken. He had believed in salmon farming, he had believed it could be done well, and that it shouldn't damage the environment. He believed it was wrong to farm salmon at Okehampton Bay but not that it was wrong to farm salmon. The more he spoke out, the more phone calls he received and the darker the threats became. It went on for months, he says. Not the old Tasmanian threats—the bullet in the mailbox, the brick through the window, the abuse on the street, the wallaby with the slit throat—but bankruptcy and character assassination.

'Corporate threats?' I ask.

'You could say that,' Armitage replied.

Threats seem to be the industry's way. Tassal's plans for Okehampton Bay provoked widespread opposition, which joined people of all classes and political beliefs—from the Hunters and Fishers Party through to the Greens—in opposition to salmon farming. Along with other east coasters, Jim Playsted—a former Liberal Party candidate and successful real estate agent who had for thirty years run machinery dealerships supplying construction, forestry and mining contractors—was a member of Marine Protection Tasmania, an organisation formed to fight Tassal's expansion. At the height of the organisation's battle to save Okehampton Bay in 2017, Playsted says Tassal trawled his group's Facebook page, making phone call after phone call to members 'in which their businesses and names were threatened if they continued to speak out'.

Playsted makes the point that the opponents of the Okehampton fish farm 'were not fringe-dwelling green activists, but mums and dads with a long history on the east coast. They felt betrayed by the arrogance of a council and a government backing an unpopular proposal with no right of appeal.' He said many were rusted-on Liberal voters who felt betrayed by the Liberal government's secrecy and manipulation of communities over salmon farming.

Playsted is not against the salmon industry but wants it properly regulated, independently monitored and out of inshore coastal waters.

'Yet successive governments of both stripes have let Big Salmon run rogue and become a sacred cow,' he says. 'Every rock you look under reveals just more secrecy and government leveraging.'

And nothing offers leverage in a small community like the threat of losing a government job or contract. Fear of Tassal is widespread in Tasmania. As one senior public servant told me, on the condition of anonymity, previous senior managers of the Department of Primary Industries, Parks, Water and Environment's (DPIPWE) Marine Farming Branch—the government overseers of the salmon industry—'had been terrified of Tassal. The salmon farmers,' this person told me, 'rule the Marine Farming Branch.'

Wayne Bell is a structural draftsman who grew up in Port Huon on the Huon River, messing about in boats, and fishing. 'There's no point fishing there now, though,' he says. 'It's just slime and no fish since fish farming took off.' Bell wrote letters to the local paper, speaking out against fish farming.

The section below has been cut for legal reasons.

Wayne Bell says he knows others who have had their jobs or businesses threatened for opposing salmon farming. I ask how they are threatened. Bell replies that they're rung and told, 'I'm going to take any business I can away from you; I'm going to ruin you; I'm going to destroy you.'

I contact person after person who tell a similar story: they 'liked' a story on Facebook that questioned fish farming, or they made a comment somewhere on social media about fish farming in a less than positive light. And subsequently they are emailed or called with threats to their business and livelihood. The fear salmon farming engenders around its activities is palpable and consequential. In the course of writing this book I have had witnesses go silent, have encountered those damaged by the industry who are gagged by NDAs, have met whistle-blowers whose testimony cannot be used.

Another example: the Tasmanian public servant who in the course of her work had cause to remonstrate with government regulators and a salmon corporation's employees about a failure to both enforce and observe regulations. This led to an email, which I have sighted, from the corporation to the woman's senior manager accusing the woman of 'gross negligence', expressing concern about the woman's 'professional and mental state', threatening 'legal action', and concluding with a warning: 'use this as a lesson—and I trust a lesson about if you put something in writing—and if it is incorrect or inappropriate—then you face the consequences'. The senior manager backed their staff against the salmon corporation.

The following year, the woman—as a local rate-payer—lodged a private objection with her local council against a planned development by the same salmon corporation. This time the corporation contacted her minister's office which in turn contacted her senior manager, who once more stood firm in support of the woman.

Four years later the public servant has asked not to be identified, as did several scientists, some for fear of losing contract work with the government or salmon industry, others working at the University of Tasmania's Institute for Marine Science and Antarctic Studies (IMAS), who fear adverse consequences should they be named, given the salmon industry's sponsorship of IMAS research.

And then there is Warwick Hastwell, a mussel farmer who in 2016 alleged on *Four Corners* that his Dover mussel farm had been destroyed by pollution from a neighbouring Tassal salmon farm, driving him out of business. Tassal denied responsibility but it bought Hastwell's mussel lease in a deal that had Hastwell agree not to speak publicly about the matter again, nor to speak disparagingly about Tassal.

Hastwell said he had no choice but to sign, given mussels could no longer be grown on his farm because of Tassal's pollution. But when Hastwell agreed to speak to a Senate inquiry into salmon farming in 2015, his lawyer allegedly received an email from Tassal, warning of Hastwell's 'obligations not to make disparaging comments to the Senate Inquiry'.[183]

Given this would amount to witness-tampering and almost certainly be in breach of the Parliamentary Privileges Act, Tassal says it never made such a statement. In a statement to the ASX Tassal claimed 'at no point did Tassal deter Mr Hastwell from appearing before the Senate Inquiry'.[184] But Hastwell chose not to appear at the inquiry, telling *Four Corners'* Caro Meldrum-Hanna this was because 'he had accepted a deal from Tassal'. He made it clear that he believed he was coerced not to appear:

Meldrum-Hanna: Do you believe that you were prevented or coerced from giving evidence at the inquiry?

Mr Hastwell: Yes.

Meldrum-Hanna: Do you have the material to back that up?

Mr Hastwell: Yes, I do.

Meldrum-Hanna: In what form is that?

Mr Hastwell: I have copies of emails and letters withdrawing the offer because of [how] it could be construed. I think they'd woken up to the fact that what they were doing was essentially illegal and they thought they better try and get out of it. But as I said, you know . . . we'd already accepted the deal.[185]

In 2017 the Senate voted to refer claims that Tassal had 'improperly influenced a witness' to its Standing Committee of Privileges (SCP). The SCP subsequently cleared Tassal—though not without reservations, including a concern that 'decisions about whether to give evidence and/or what evidence a witness might give should not be used as currency in commercial negotiations'.[186]

When it comes to Tasmanian salmon, money doesn't talk—it silences. The use of contracts to buy the silence of those who feel they have had their lives devastated has proven to be a well-tried and successful tactic by the salmon industry.

Like Warwick Hastwell, it would appear that sixth-generation farmer Peter Headlam and his son James have had much of what they value about their life, home and work destroyed after Tassal announced plans to build Australia's largest fish hatchery next door to their family farm, Sendace, at Hamilton in the Derwent Valley.

James Headlam and his family lived in the original soldier-settler house on Sendace. For years they had dreamt of a new home on their farm. In July 2019 Headlam submitted plans to his local council for this new family house. Two months later Tassal submitted plans for an industrial facility, to be built 450 metres from the Headlam's proposed new home. Tassal subsequently opposed Headlam's plans.

For the Headlams, the nightmare had begun. They discovered their paradisiacal world was about to be turned upside down. What was in effect a giant factory operating round the clock in which millions of fish fry were to be bathed in soups of everything from formaldehyde to antibiotics was now to dominate their lives. And with it would come the associated odours, lights, noise and a parade of heavy trucks going back and forth all day and all night, as well as giant pumps ceaselessly and noisily sucking up water from Meadowbank Lake, one of several hydro-electric impoundments on the Derwent River—Hobart's principal water catchment.

When the Headlams began to look at Tassal's plans in detail, they realised what was being proposed raised many questions that did not seem to have been adequately answered, far less addressed by the salmon company.[187] Like Warwick Hastwell before them, the Headlams went public with their opposition and their concerns.

The hatchery would recycle its water rather than relying on the older flow-through systems of other Tasmanian salmon hatcheries. While an advance on the older technology, this method would still produce, annually, 158 megalitres of highly concentrated effluent, which would be stored in a containment dam and, mixed with freshwater, used to fertilise pasture with pivot irrigators.

What would seem a neat solution to the problem of pollution foundered on the completely inappropriate siting of the hatchery so close to Meadowbank Lake. Despite the lake having a very high conservation status, despite its purity being essential for Hobart's drinking water, despite the massive pollution problems the other salmon hatcheries were already creating by contaminating Hobart's drinking water, another giant hatchery was being built right next to the lake. The Derwent River, like the Channel and Huon, like Bruny Island, like the Tasman Peninsula, like Macquarie Harbour, like Storm Bay, like Okehampton, was to become one more sacrificial zone for the salmon industry's avarice.

When the Headlams pointed out that the planned containment dam for the hatchery's toxic effluent, only 850 metres away from Meadowbank Lake, risked overflow during storms, with the runoff spilling into Hobart's drinking water catchment, this concern was dismissed by both Tassal and the EPA.[188]

Like Warwick Hastwell, the Headlams discovered the government processes and representatives from various departments seemed to accord them no rights, and yet seemed to do everything to accelerate Tassal's plans through a charade of processes.

Even worse than the possibility of that occasional catastrophe was the potential for the ongoing pollution of Hobart's drinking water from runoff containing the effluent being used as irrigation. It was a concern made in objections by locals when Tassal's hatchery was assessed for approval by the Central Highlands Council. 'Unfortunately the reality of irrigation is that run-off will occur to some degree,' wrote one. Others pointed to the issues of leaching, runoff and spray drift of the recycled water.[189] James Headlam tried to raise the alarm publicly. 'There was always runoff from irrigation water,' he told the ABC, 'and it was going to be out of Tassal's control.'[190]

The problem at Hamilton would be worsened by the poor water retention of the local soil and compounded by the undulating topography of the areas to be irrigated, with some parts becoming saturated before others, making runoff not just inevitable but necessary in order to irrigate the whole. As a farmer with intimate knowledge of the land where the concentrated effluent dam was to be built, James Headlam knew 'all pivots produce enough water for runoff . . . which ultimately ends up in the lake'. And the lake was from where local farmers, including the Headlams, drew their own drinking water.

We have seen how the nitrate and phosphorous pollution from salmon hatcheries led to costly algal blooms in Hobart's drinking water catchments prior to the approval of the giant Hamilton hatchery. But the Headlams faced a worse risk with their own drinking water. In the absence of any overall monitoring of nitrate pollution in the Derwent by the Tasmanian regulators, Tasmanians can only assume that the increasing combined nitrate pollution from the salmon hatcheries will remain sufficiently diluted in Hobart's main source of drinking water to avoid the many ways in which nitrate-contaminated drinking water can seriously impact human health.[191] Because if it were not sufficiently diluted; if nitrate pollution in Hobart's drinking water catchment continues to be permitted by authorities to increase rather than being reduced; if old salmon hatcheries are permitted by regulators to continue growing; if new hatcheries are licensed to allow for the doubling of production that the government has ordained—then there would be grounds for the most serious concern.

A US study using data from the National Birth Defects Prevention Study found a positive association between prenatal consumption of drinking water with higher levels of nitrates and cases of spina bifida, limb deficiency, cleft palate and cleft lip.[192] Nitrate-contaminated drinking water has also been linked to 'blue baby syndrome' (methaemoglobinaemia)[193] while a Slovakian epidemiologic study found higher nitrate levels in drinking water were associated with increased cases of stomach cancer, colorectal cancer, non-Hodgkin lymphoma and overall cancer for women, and more colorectal cancer and non-Hodgkin lymphoma in men.[194]

The Headlams could not understand why—when the hatchery could be built a safe distance away—Tassal would build a factory with a highly polluted water output right next to Hobart's major drinking water catchment with a risk of further contaminating that drinking water. Yet that was exactly what Tassal was doing with full EPA approval.

'The past history of decisions made by the EPA re finfish production do not give me much confidence in the chance of no foreseeable negative impacts,' Peter Headlam wrote in a despairing submission to the Legislative Council. 'I do not need to reiterate the disasters of Macquarie Harbour or the D'Entrecasteaux Channel.'[195]

This, after all, was the same EPA that had from 2016 presided over the environmental catastrophe of Macquarie Harbour, making excuses and refusing to act for years; where regulation was so entirely absent that one salmon corporation had to sue the government in the hope of having the EPA enforce the rules.[196]

Tassal's four other hatcheries on the Derwent system were described to me by a scientist with experience of the aquaculture industry as 'representing a massive series of sewage farms'. A dirty secret of Tasmanian aquaculture is that the dams on the Derwent River—popular with trout fishermen—are now effectively used as secondary treatment ponds for much of the salmon industry's immense output of sewage.

What the Headlams came to see was that the risk to Hobart's drinking water and trout fishermen was significantly increased by Tassal's new hatchery in ways that the EPA refused to recognise. In its role of enabling the salmon industry at the expense of Tasmania's people, the EPA doesn't ask the questions that matter. It chooses neither to measure nor regulate the combined impact of *all* hatcheries on the Derwent system with regard to nutrient enrichment as well as antibiotics, hormones and other chemicals.

In another world, Tassal would be able to offer up solid evidence that there is no risk from its Hamilton hatchery, and, with it, a bond to show good faith if things did not work out as Tassal had promised they would. Tassal would be able to explain what it is doing to check its *combined* impact on Hobart's water supply. And the EPA would be able to reassure Tasmanians with strong evidence that clearly demonstrates the combined pollution from the hatcheries is *not* posing a risk to the ecology of the Derwent River, its trout fisheries and the quality of its drinking water. But as the Headlams learnt, this was not another world.

Peter Headlam described Tassal's way of gaining approval for their hatchery as 'divisive and underhand', 'such that the general public were kept in the dark'. 'Dismissive' he went on, 'is understating Tassal's approach.' Their 'bullying tactics ... when dealing with the local community' were, he wrote, 'an entrenched attitude' within Tassal.[197]

His submission to the Legislative Council was made on 29 November 2019. Five days later Tassal won approval to build its hatchery. Once more, Tassal's 'entrenched attitude' had triumphed, at the expense of people's lives and with substantial environmental and human health risk.

What subsequently happened to the Headlam family is unknown. When I contacted Peter in late

2020 to ask if he might be willing to talk about his experience, I received a polite reply saying his son had reached an agreement with Tassal that was 'subject to a confidentiality agreement. This prevents me from further comments as to the impact of the Tassal hatchery on our farm'.

Like Warwick Hastwell, it would seem that having had their lives and hopes for the future ruined, the Headlams were offered some sort of deal by Tassal to stop them continuing to tell their story. Like the ever-growing mound of fish faeces, uneaten food and writhing white worms, the increasing number of fish-farm death zones, theirs was just one more story that could be left to sink out of sight, with all the other secrets, far below the water line where no one would ever see it.

But nothing stays hidden forever.

In recent times, key executives and directors at such major companies as Rio Tinto, AMP and QBE have all lost their jobs when corporate and individual behaviour were met with community disapproval. As respected corporate affairs journalist Adele Ferguson recently noted, 'The days where companies could get away with blaming systemic failures or flawed corporate governance on a few bad apples, errors and other lame excuses dreamt up by PR teams are all but over. We are now operating in a world where trust has been broken and communities will no longer put up with companies that operate in the dark and feast on opacity.'[198]

In such a rapidly changing climate, the boards of the salmon corporations would be wise to be on notice. The two major Tasmanian salmon corporations—Tassal, with a market capitalisation in 2019 of $885 million, and Huon Aquaculture, with a valuation of $394 million— are publicly listed companies, with environmental and social records that crack further open the more they are closely scrutinised.[199] Tassal is a company with a record of cover-up and denial, which shows consistent bad faith in its dealings with affected communities. Its environmental record is appalling. The company is consistently singled out for claims of bullying, intimidation and threats. With the recent turmoil over sexual harassment at AMP culminating in the resig- nation of its CEO, with Rio Tinto investors calling for 'true accountability' in the wake of its destruction of priceless global heritage, there is a discernible shift in investor sentiment.

Since the Hayne Royal Commission into Misconduct in the Banking, Superannuation and Financial Services Industry, the issue of corporate culture at the highest levels has been a significant issue for shareholders and corporate boards. Commissioner Hayne specifically called out the 'cultural drivers of misconduct', with explosive ramifications throughout Australia's corporate world.[200]

'For too long corporate Australia has been allowed to get away with practices that might be legal but are unethical and immoral,' Ferguson writes. 'It became clear that poor behaviour damages brands and reputations which, in turn, hurts an organisation's bottom line.'[201]

'How a company manages its approach to environmental, social and governance issues in its operations—is now more than analyst jargon,' Brynn O'Brien, the executive director of the Australasian Centre for Corporate Responsibility, recently wrote in the *Australian Financial Review*. 'Social licence . . . is vital to the creation and protection of shareholder value.'[202]

'In the end,' Peter George, co-chairperson of the Tasmanian Alliance for Marine Protection (TAMP), Tasmania's peak marine conservation body, told me, 'it's the bottom line: if the salmon smell, they won't sell.'

And the stench rising from the dark waters beneath Tasmania's salmon farms grows with every passing day.

7

FLOATING JUST ON THE SURFACE, THICK AS A footballer's thigh, full of seawater and sometimes weighing tonnes, the great lengths of rigid black plastic pipe are difficult to sight before collision, at which point they can rear up and come flying over the boat, bringing it to a sudden, terrifying halt and risking injury and even death to those on board. The debris is piping lost from salmon farms. After an abalone diver hit a 150-metre length of Tassal polypipe near Dover in August 2016, injuring himself and badly damaging his boat, Peter Hopkins, the manager of Marine and Safety Tasmania (MAST), wrote an email to Tassal, Huon Aquaculture and the Tasmanian government's Marine Farming Branch.

'I guess it is another case of gear literally floating "around" and no one taking responsibility until something happens,' Hopkins wrote. 'Seriously, someone will get killed soon ... It's time your respective companies took some responsibility and MFB [Marine Farming Branch] had some plans in place to manage all this and show some social conscience. A coroner would rip this industry apart if a fatality occurred after our warnings.'[203]

In spite of his warnings, in spite of Tasmania having the largest boating population in Australia, with one in seventeen Tasmanians owning a boat and one in eight having a boating licence, accident after accident continues to occur.[204] In February 2020 Jarrod Nation hit drifting Tassal polypipe in his boat in Mercury Passage as he motored through the water at 50 kilometres an hour. His boat sustained $60,000 worth of damage, for which Tassal was fined just $680.[205] Another collision in Storm Bay a few months later, when a boat owner was on the water with his family and travelling at about 25 knots, led the owner to reiterate on ABC radio what Peter Hopkins had warned four years earlier: someone was going to die because of the problem of the salmon farms' plastic pollution.[206]

The salmon industry's massive floating feedlots are built out of thousands of tonnes of plastic: huge, rigid plastic pipe scaffolding up to half a metre in diameter, plastic netting, plastic pulleys, plastic stanchions, plastic handrails, plastic walkways, kilometres of nylon rope. In consequence, Tasmania's south-east coast is now plagued with plastic pollution.

Littering formerly beautiful beaches and pristine coastline is plastic detritus lost or discarded from fish farms: everything from massive construction pipes—which, when not washed ashore, drift dark and unseen on the surface of the sea—to nylon ropes, plastic writing boards, plastic switches, trestles, netting, feed bags, dye bags, black plastic detritus of a hundred different forms and shapes—steps, grates, barrels, buoys—through to the seemingly endless swarf, the name given to fine black plastic shavings, chips and twists from repairs to the farms' plastic infrastructure, which turns up everywhere.

Like everything else about the salmon industry, what is visible is only a fraction of what is hidden in the ocean. Those who wonder about the resulting microplastic pollution as the plastic degrades in the most popular recreational fisheries in Tasmania—fearing the problem may be immense—are kept wondering. With Trumpian logic, the salmon industry understands that if you don't test, you don't find. Microplastic pollution is yet one more area of salmon farming's environmental impacts that is neither monitored nor scientifically measured or regulated. Rather, there is the normal empty rhetoric from government about general marine farm plastic pollution, claiming it has a zero-tolerance approach to the matter, and tough penalties, while the industry asserts it has a vigorous clean-up campaign.

In reality, communities continue to do much of the onshore cleaning up, boats keep hitting plastic, and microplastics proliferate—one more unseen, unspoken tragedy of the commons. The salmon companies seem more interested in cleaning up their image by, for example, signing up boat owners who have had collisions with debris to non-disclosure agreements in return for paying for their repairs, which can run into tens of thousands of dollars.

The hypocrisy around this plastic pollution is typical of the regulatory failure at the heart of the Tasmanian salmon industry. Lax regulation has created huge crises for the industry in other countries, being blamed for the near-total collapse of Chile's salmon industry in 2008 as well as for a recent major fall in production in Scotland. Norway, on the other hand, where salmon farming was first developed, is far more strongly regulated, with producers paying substantial sums in licence fees.[207]

If Tasmania were to switch to the Norwegian auction system, it would see the return to the Tasmanian people increasing from less than $1 million a year to somewhere between $707 million and $2 billion.[208] In the view of Dr Torbjorn Forseth, head of the scientific committee that advises the Norwegian government on regulating the salmon industry, 'the farming industry needs regulation to operate properly'. According to Arnfinn Torgnes, head of the Norwegian Aquaculture

Centre, 'We need to have a Big Brother watching you that we don't do anything that's not good for ourselves and also for the fish [*sic*].'[209]

But in Tasmania, when it comes to government regulation, it's less a case of Big Brother above, and more the servants downstairs. The subservience of government to industry is on public display at Hobart's Marine Board building. Tassal's headquarters in the eleven-storey office block is on level nine. Six floors beneath is the Marine Farming Branch of the state government. Ostensibly charged with overseeing and licensing Big Salmon, the Marine Farming Branch offices and officers give every appearance of existing only to enable, promote, protect and defend the increasingly indefensible acts of those who reside above.

The origins of such deference go back more than thirty years, when, as Australia rebounded after the early 1980s recession, Tasmania stagnated under successive governments that were committed to propping up old resource industries such as mining and logging, no matter the environmental damage and economic fallout. As Australia changed, Tasmania fell further behind. For the Robin Gray-led Liberal state government in the wake of their historic defeat over the Franklin Dam issue, salmon farming seemed to offer an old resource industry in a newly acceptable disguise.

Far from being a prudent regulator balancing social, environmental and economic concerns, the Tasmanian government was instead the industry's principal developer and protagonist. Through an act of parliament in 1985 the Gray government established Salmon Enterprises of Tasmania (Saltas) as Tasmania's first salmon-producing company, with the Tasmanian government itself as the majority owner.[210] From the beginning, state interest and corporate profit were seen to be one and the same by politicians, bureaucrats and business, with the boundary between private advantage and public interest non-existent, creating what would develop over the next thirty years into a toxic culture.

According to a former senior Tasmanian public servant, who has asked to remain anonymous—in an account confirmed by a second source—the Norwegian consultants who helped establish the industry in the mid-1980s advised the Tasmanian government that, other than in one or two experimental pens, salmon farming could never be allowed in D'Entrecasteaux Channel. The Channel was too shallow and its flow too weak to disperse the thousands upon thousands of tonnes of sludge that the farms would produce and, in consequence, farming would be ruinous to those waterways and its marine ecosystems. That advice was ignored. D'Entrecasteaux Channel and the even shallower Huon Estuary are to this day the Tasmanian salmon industry's ground zero, with inestimable damage in consequence.

For an industry that hypes itself as world's best practice, its methods have always been more third world than first, lagging far behind those of Europe. As Mark Kurlansky points out in his 2020 study of European salmon farming, nets need to be placed in deep water and 'should have more than 30 metres of swiftly moving ocean current flowing beneath them'.[211] Yet the total depths in Tasmania's shallow inshore farms, from sea floor to surface, rarely *exceed* 30 metres, with nets sitting close to the sea floor in sluggish water, creating marine death zones beneath every salmon farm that are fully legal under Tasmania's slack regulations. What the Norwegians predicted has come to pass: pointing to the destruction of their marine ecosystems, community groups on Bruny Island and along the Huon are now calling for the salmon farmers to quit their waterways.

The sludge pouring out of the floating feedlots in the form of fish faeces, uneaten food and ammonia can destroy marine ecosystems by overloading them with excess nutrients. As the table overleaf shows, the huge amount of dissolved nitrogen flooding into D'Entrecasteaux Channel and the Huon alone from salmon farms is now close to three times that produced by Tasmania's total sewage load. When maximum production is reached in Storm Bay, the total dissolved nitrogen load from all salmon farms will be over 8000 tonnes—or almost ten times the dissolved nitrogen released from all of Tasmania's sewage works.

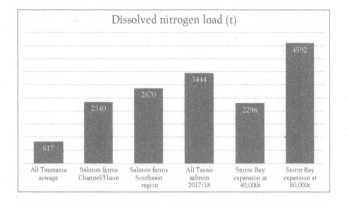

Source: Derwent Estuary Program Submission on Storm Bay Marine Farming Development Plan, 2018, p. 3

The catastrophic impacts of nutrient overload that laid waste to Macquarie Harbour are now a tragedy that threatens to befall D'Entrecasteaux Channel, the Huon and places such as Long Bay, adjacent to the Port Arthur World Heritage Site. Disturbing videos made by community groups such as Neighbours of Fish Farming show the smothering of once pristine marine ecosystems by pollution-fed algae. The footage shows divers appearing out of, and vanishing back into, filthy murk, while seaweed and kelp is being choked by tuft algae. There are no fish.[212]

'The flathead are gone and the seabed is a desert,' Gerard Castles, Friends of North Bruny vice-president, recently said, when North Bruny Island community groups called on Tassal to leave the Channel. 'What was once rich with marine life is now slimed with algae from their pollution, frequently full of jellyfish and little else.'[213]

'We could do something about it,' as Tasmanian scientist Lisa-ann Gershwin has said, 'if only we bothered to notice . . . The species are still there to be recorded during surveys, but their reduced numbers function as mere ghosts in an ecosystem that is essentially the walking dead, just waiting for inevitable collapse.'[214]

Though the salmon industry seems a story of corporate greed, the real story is one of a failure of governance that is the industry's original sin. For at its start the salmon industry was only about politics, and it was created and driven by politicians who knew the long-term damage it would cause, but chose to ignore their own experts' advice. By the 1990s government was well aware that salmon farming damaged coastal ecology, affecting water quality and 'causing excessive growth of toxic algae'.[215] But instead of working to reduce these problems, it did the opposite.

'The substantial ministerial discretion is no doubt intended to promote the development of the [salmon] industry,' concluded the federal government's Productivity Commission in 1996. 'But the process is not transparent and like all non-transparent administrative processes may be open to accusations of bias.'[216] At every step, when the industry faltered and companies teetered—and for nearly two decades the salmon industry continued failing—even while community opposition arose and found success halting farms in public opposition and through law courts, successive Tasmanian governments expended great effort in keeping the unpopular industry afloat with legislation, subsidies, rescue packages, and loans.[217] From support for research and development, export development grants, loan guarantees, and even buying direct equity in salmon companies such as the recurrently failing Tassal, to promote 'investor confidence', coupled to a lax, entirely inadequate regulatory regime, the government again and again ensured a floundering industry survived.[218]

As Tasmania's economy worsened through the 1990s, the only state in the history of federation to experience a net loss of population, both Liberal and Labor politicians targeted salmon farming alongside mining and forestry, seeing a resource revival as the island's only hope—even though it was exactly this determined political support for these industries at the expense of others that was holding back the state's economy. Large swathes of inshore coastal waterways alongside communities— loved and popular with locals, adjacent to important commercial and recreational fisheries—were given away for new salmon farms, the government slashing rent for marine farming leases in 1998 to the ludicrous sum of $200 a hectare of public waters, privatising the common waters for almost no public return. All this, and with minimal scientific research to back it up.[219]

What happened next is best explained by Chris Wells, a national aquaculture planner who worked on the Eyre Peninsula Aquaculture Development Plan and a catchment-to-coast plan for the far south of New South Wales. According to Wells, there was never any serious attempt in Tasmania 'to address site selection criteria such as water depth, water movement, fallowing to enable dispersal of nutrients loaded from farming activity. Instead, legislation was passed fast-tracking salmon farming development and bypassing normal planning processes. This very poor start to the industry did not immediately cause problems in the environment because farms were small, pens were small and stocking densities limited. Leases were granted in areas of little tidal movement that were conveniently located for business owners and the business of salmon farming began.

'As years went by, pens became larger, biomass of fish increased, and companies listed on the ASX ... The marine environments were compromised by large-scale farming, overstocking became the norm to increase profits, and the regulators at DPIPWE and later the EPA turned a blind eye to the problems.'[220]

Tasmania's long history of well-documented corruption of politics by major industries such as forestry and gambling—and its lack of an ICAC—means Tasmanians survive in a culture where the expectation is that the system is corrupted. Whichever party ostensibly reigns, few expect their government to govern for anyone but the powerful.

The years passed, the salmon companies grew, and so too their reputation for bullying, deceit and environmental rapacity, while the Tasmanian polity and bureaucracy grew craven to its demon child. The rule of law that existed for ordinary Tasmanians did not seem to exist in any real sense for the salmon industry, and such laws that did exist were honoured only by neglect. The Tasmanian people were left to live the consequences.

Even when the salmon companies were found to have committed criminal acts—such as the recently uncovered scandal of Tassal's illegal caging of seals in 2016—the Tasmanian government worked to ensure they evaded prosecution. In a state where bureaucrats seem to make their careers serving salmon corporations rather than the laws of parliament, regulation is not enforcing the law but enabling and excusing crimes. As Guy Barnett, the Primary Industries minister responsible for fish farming, put it when talking about the government's spirited actions to help Tassal escape criminal prosecution: 'The department processes were appropriate.'[221]

In this, Tasmanian politicians were replicating the crony capitalism that characterised the bad days of Gunns, the logging monopoly that poisoned the state's polity for more than twenty years. Even the conservative, Murdoch-owned Hobart *Mercury* recognised 'the parallel between the Government's treatment of aquaculture and of forestry. In both cases there is lack of transparency, noncritical political support and over-zealous legislative protection.'[222]

After the unique ecology of Macquarie Harbour was wrecked by Tassal's greed, no fines were ever issued nor meaningful reforms of the regulatory system made. Far from it: the salmon industry, having demonstrated supreme irresponsibility and a commitment to profit no matter the environmental damage, was rewarded with the opening up of a vast new area in south-east Tasmania for expansion: Storm Bay. As Louise Cherrie and Professor Nowak were to learn, that was because the salmon industry wanted Storm Bay, and what the salmon industry wanted, the salmon industry got.

And yet the more scientists and communities point to everything that is wrong with the salmon industry, and the growing environmental tragedy that the industry drives, the more Tasmanian Liberal and Labor politicians refuse to acknowledge anything is. Politicians' defences of such outrages always begin with claims of the industry's centrality to the island's economy and employment. Tassal boasted to the 2019 Tasmanian parliamentary inquiry into the industry that it is 'one of the largest employers in Tasmania', one more untruth without foundation in reality, but one regularly echoed by politicians.[223] According to the 2019 Australia Institute report, the Tasmanian salmon industry was the fortieth largest sector by employment in Tasmania, with only 0.6 per cent of the population—or 1500 employees—the same number of Tasmanians who work at making 'bakery products'.[224] In other words, ninety-nine out of a hundred Tasmanians do *not* work for Big Salmon.

To put these numbers into greater context, prior to COVID, Federal Group, a tourist and gaming chain, employed more than 2000 people, while tourism supported 42,000 jobs or 17.2 per cent of total Tasmanian employment, contributing 10.3 per cent to gross state product (GSP). The salmon industry, on the other hand, employed less than 1 per cent of the state's workers, and contributed somewhere between

1 and 2 per cent to Tasmania's GSP, making a mockery
of the government's Marine Farming Branch claim
that salmon farming is one of Tasmania's 'major
industries'.[225]

Along with 'world's best practice', such assertions
are evidence only of an industry and a government
that long ago came to believe the salmon corporations'
hyperbolic marketing as reality in defiance of truth.

And yet every new push for more common waters
to be annexed and enclosed by the salmon industry
is justified by the jobs it will supposedly create. But,
again, the evidence suggests that the growth of the
salmon industry does not drive growth in jobs. In
1994–95 the industry produced 7000 tonnes of salmon
and employed the equivalent of 570 full-time staff
members.[226] Twenty-two years later, the industry had
increased production by more than 800 per cent, to
60,000 tonnes, but employment had not even tripled
to 1600 fulltime jobs.[227] While the industry increased
production by 50 per cent between 2013 and 2018, with
profits similarly soaring, employment appears to have
stayed constant as the salmon companies, far from
investing in growing employment, invested heavily
in job *shedding*, high technology and heavy industrial
infrastructure—from robotic net cleaners to central-
ised computerised feed systems controlling multiple
farms from remote centres, to the introduction of the

gigantic factory ships. Each of these transformations saw significant reductions in the farms' less skilled workforce.

Many more fish may equal more profit. But it will mean very few new jobs.

As the industry embarks on its greatest acceleration ever, with its planned doubling over the next decade, much will be promised in the way of jobs. But if Scotland is anything to go by, we can expect very few to eventuate. There, where in 2019 production increased by 30.7 per cent to 203,881 tonnes—or well over three times Tasmania's total production—employment in 'marine salmon production' reached 1651 jobs.[228]

The salmon farmers' last line of defence on jobs is their claim to be major employers in depressed regional areas, but as a submission made by the Huon Valley Council to the Tasmanian parliament in 2019 made clear—in addition to highlighting various environmental concerns—less educated locals 'struggled to get jobs with aquaculture companies because they lacked the skills'. Under pressure from Huon Aquaculture, the council withdrew their submissions.[229]

This is not to say the salmon industry is insignificant. But while it is the largest commercial fishery in Australia, it is employment-lite, and its technology-intensive, heavy industrial model pushes its costs on to communities and the environment. A 2021 report by London-based Just Economics found that globally salmon farming cost US$47 billion between 2013 and 2019 through the damage it was wreaking on marine ecosystems with pollution, parasites and high fish mortality rates.[230] Meanwhile, investor red lights are flashing globally that salmon companies, as they come up against their environmental limits, need to transition into more sustainable environmental practices as a matter of urgency.[231]

The glittering story of success Big Salmon spins around itself hasn't persuaded the stock market, where these days Australian salmon corporations make at best average return for their investors, with share prices far from their past heights. In February 2021, Huon Aquaculture posted a half-year statutory loss of $95.3 million, its shares were trading at record lows, down over 50 per cent from their peak in 2017, and it was being reported as a potential takeover target.[232] At the same time, Tassal had 12 per cent of its shares shorted, making it the second-most shorted company listed on the ASX. Shorting is a technique used by traders in order to profit from a fall in stock price: companies are 'targeted because of clearly-flagged recent problems'.[233] As such it offers an insight into what the market is thinking about a company's future prospects. Shorting is the stock market equivalent of the vultures circling.

Given the small material return from the industry to Tasmania, and the increasing evidence of its profound damage, anger among many Tasmanians grows. Outside the handful of small towns in which salmon farming offers some jobs, the industry has few friends other than Labor and Liberal apparatchiks and a handful of senior public servants whose careers have been bound up in their fealty to salmon company CEOs. Communities across south-east Tasmania want the farmers out of their waters. No Tasmanian community welcomes new salmon farms. The King Island community fought a powerful and ultimately successful campaign to stop farms being established there.

When newly elected Tasmanian upper house member independent Meg Webb managed in 2019 to get up the parliamentary inquiry into the state's salmon industry, witness after witness came forward to tell the story of the ongoing trails of destruction wrought by the industry. There emerged distressingly similar stories: people living in Tasmania's coastal areas, loved for their beauty and serenity, seeing these areas destroyed when fish farmers arrived.

In submission after submission they described the eruption of algal blooms in previously pristine waters; the sliming of once clean, rocky shorelines; the fouling of inlet after bay after beach. The vanishing of native fish. The growing sense of something vast and irrecoverable being lost and no one seeing it. The continuous throb of diesel engines, the lights shining into people's houses, the windows rattling, the pictures on the walls shaking. The corrupted processes of government. The deep, sickening cynicism of the salmon corporations' responses, which in their marketing to Australian consumers boast of 'Our Communities', claiming ordinary Tasmanians as one more aspect of their stolen property. And underlying it their own powerlessness and loss of agency when having borne witness they are confronted with government and corporation, politician and salmon farmer and bureaucrat firmly fixed on denying them the truth of their loss.

'Our heart place,' is how Michelle Pears described Stingaree Bay. 'Our beautiful bays are struggling once again with Algae Growth choking the once lush seagrass beds and seaweeds. Brown silt covers the bottom of the bay. Slimy islands of green/yellow algae float in the sheltered areas of both Stingaree and Long Bay.'[234]

'I have been a diver for 45 years and in that time I have witnessed the destruction of our marine environment with my own eyes,' Christo Lees told the inquiry. 'The salmon industry has destroyed the Channel region . . . Once pristine sandy bottoms are now mud and covered by slimy weed and clean weed beds are covered in fine sediment and most native fish have disappeared.'[235]

'Tassal does nothing, the Kelp is gone, no Sea birds feed in this side of the bay where water depth is low, ducks are gone . . . and so many others,' wrote Denis Mermet of Port Arthur. 'That shouldn't be allowed to happen. Our Bay is dying.'[236]

'I am 89 years of age,' Mabs Mollineaux wrote. 'My family history on the Tasman Peninsula goes back to convict times . . . There were 3 pretty little beaches, white with lovely shell grit for my Gran's chickens and plentiful fish (including plenty of crayfish and flounder). When my 4 children came along they spent a lot of time on the bay with their dinghies, paddle boards and canoes . . . Many hundreds, if not thousands of young Tasmanians have spent time in this spot, enjoying Long Bay and Stingaree Bay.

'In the mid 80's the salmon farm moved in and the beautiful white sands turned grey . . . things have become a disaster. The beaches have blackish sludge, the top of the water is putrid with this sludge (stinking), killing the beautiful seagrass below. No longer do our beautiful bays sparkle. Sadly our beautiful bays are almost dead.'[237]

'Our beach has been regularly afflicted with slimy rocks and an unpleasant-looking foam, reminiscent of stagnant water,' wrote Alan Kemp and Lisa Litjens of the Huon's Petcheys Bay. 'Additionally, there has been salmon pen litter washed up on the beach: large plastic bags, water pipes and even a huge marker buoy. For the first few months we regularly heard what sounded like rifle shots coming from the pens. We were told they were seal scaring shots. Our near neighbour, a keen rod fisherman, laments that the majority of fish he now catches look diseased and discoloured.'[238]

'We don't fish here anymore. No fish,' Lynda House of Middleton, in the heart of the Channel country, wrote. 'Our boat has not been in the water for about 2 and a half years . . . Living here can seem like you are living next to a factory. My family has seen the disintegration of the health of the Channel while diving . . . The seaweed has suffered, the bed of the Channel is barren in places, especially close to the fish farms . . . the channel is destroyed.'[239]

Chris Wells, a recreational angler, described how twenty years ago 'there was a terrific seatrout fishery in the Lune and Esperance rivers . . . Each spring the trout would follow the whitebait migrations. The rivers were tannin stained but clean. The pebbles clearly defined on the river bottoms. In twenty years the nutrient loading from the adjacent farms has destroyed the whitebait runs, the trout no longer run and the river bottoms are covered in a green-brown scum . . . It is observable to anyone who has seen these rivers deteriorate so markedly as the fish farms have expanded.'[240]

'I am an amateur diver and dive for abalone, crayfish and scallops,' testified Tony Mahood of Middleton. '12 years ago there was hardly any algae underwater and today it is so bad that when you dive, the algae is continually wrapping around your face.'[241]

'Fish Farms are creating dirty water not fit for me to swim in off Big Roaring Beach,' wrote Susan Westcott of the Tasmanian Peninsula. 'An increase in algae and a change in visible shellfish has been observed through time. There has been both noise and visual pollution with increasing search light interference . . . An unspoilt wilderness has been turned into an industrial area . . . The fish farming industry . . . [is] reducing people to a silent witness of loss of habitat for the sea creatures they love to see and loss of enjoyment for themselves and their families and future generations.'[242]

What these silent witnesses were naming was a vast crime: the taking of something for private profit that belonged to all, human and non-human alike.

'No less than the wilderness areas of the South West, the waters of Storm Bay are common, public property which has inherent value for its wildness,' wrote Bruny Islanders Simon Allston and Janeil Hall of the enormous expansion alongside Bruny Island's east coast, making the point that applies equally to salmon farming's rapacious, unchecked greed everywhere: 'It is not right that essentially unbridled development of this common property should take place, regardless of the harm done to the environment and public amenity.'[243]

And yet that is exactly what is happening in Tasmania to make Atlantic salmon.

8

FROM THE BEGINNING, TASMANIAN SALMON was an elaborate and highly successful con job. Imagine this: a small workshop that keeps failing is only saved from bankruptcy by the government continually bailing it out, and is then given the city's most-loved park on which to build a factory. The largely automated factory, filthy and noisy, never delivers the jobs that are promised. When it's found also to have poisoned the surrounding suburbs, the owners, instead of being sanctioned, ask for, and are given, another public park for another factory—and another, and another—along with government subsidies to help them profit from and poison the lives of more people.

That's the strange, improbable premise on which the Tasmanian salmon industry is built.

For the salmon industry to flourish, beloved common waters, which were also unique marine worlds, were taken from the people and transformed into private profit and industrial wastes. When wrong-doing was exposed, the salmon companies were never punished nor their industry reformed. Rather, they were rewarded with more public waters. For decades Tasmanians were expected to bear mute witness to the accelerating destruction of one extraordinary waterway after another. Those who spoke out could expect threats and intimidation from the powerful. And now, on these foundations, the Tasmanian salmon industry—with the enthusiastic support of the state government—intends to double production by 2030.

While the immediate horror of an oil spill or chemical disaster is easy to grasp, industrial food production is far slower in its impacts, but finally equally as catastrophic. It took decades for the salmon industry to scale up to such an extent that it could destroy large waterways. But today that is what is happening.

When I spoke with leading marine scientist Professor Graham Edgar, he pointed out that simply measuring nutrient levels—a key way Tasmanian regulators have to ascertain the health of marine ecosystems around salmon farms—is inadequate because it is instantaneous. And because large quantities of excess nutrients can be quickly sucked up by algae, they can escape this measurement.

He gives the example of a ship carrying phosphorus fertiliser that sank off Esperance in Western Australia.

Within several days, the 30,000 tonnes of lost fertiliser could not be detected in water samples, yet for weeks afterwards seaweeds bloomed. Professor Edgar points to the once extraordinary ecological richness of D'Entrecasteaux Channel, sites such as Tinderbox that only a few decades ago contained hundreds of small crustacean species (known as amphipods)—'More,' he says, 'than had been discovered in Britain in the last five hundred years,' and other sites that were 'in the top one per cent of sites globally for invertebrate and seaweed richness'. Professor Edgar believes that the Channel ecosystem is now very badly degraded.

Tasmanian salmon corporations' immense technology and advanced science is not concerned, though, with keeping alive the astonishing variety of invertebrates at which Graham Edgar once marvelled, nor to sustain the ecological richness of this or that marine ecosystem. They exist only to create a highly artificial, chromosomally manipulated, dyed, fatty protein with decreasing omega-3 levels. Their purpose is to fatten fish as fast as possible in an alien environment in which these fish cannot otherwise survive. They serve to make profits.

That is all.

It would take the sum of hundreds of small changes and the compounding consequences of incremental but inexorable growth for the immense damage the industry was doing to become apparent. And by then, the companies would be too big, the politicians too weak, the bureaucrats too cowed, the silence around the industry's many failings maintained by threats, bullying and legal trickery. What it would add up to was the collapse of Macquarie Harbour, the sickness of the Channel and the Huon, the catastrophe of Storm Bay and the desecration of Bruny Island, transformations we all saw too late.

The perversity is staggering. If a bushwalker intentionally lit a fire in a Tasmanian national park, destroying unique, publicly owned lands, they would risk up to twenty-one years in jail as an arsonist.[244] So how can it be that when a salmon corporation similarly destroys unique, publicly owned waters, it is rewarded with more publicly owned waters to destroy? How can it be that it can destroy World Heritage Areas—as it has in Macquarie Harbour—without consequence?

Claims of environmental responsibility on the part of the industry, of salmon being a clean and green product, ring hollow when measured against decades of a contempt for the environment so casual as to defy adequate summary.

Take the extremely rare red handfish. Its close relative, the smooth handfish, was officially declared extinct in 2020, the first fish species anywhere in the world in modern history to be declared so. Its passing is, in its way, a tragedy more terrible than that of the thylacine. Like the smooth handfish, the red handfish is unique, ancient and only found in the shallow coastal waters of south-east Tasmania. Critically endangered, it is another extraordinary creature for which Tasmania is a final refuge. There, in spite of everything pitted against it, it has managed to survive. But its population is believed, at the beginning of 2021, to number no more than eighty fish.

In 2018, only a few short years after the Tasmanian salmon industry, in its relentless greed, had driven another endangered species, the maugean skate, closer to extinction in Macquarie Harbour, Huon Aquaculture—in order to protect its remaining salmon stock from possible fatal infection—moved 5000 tonnes of live salmon that had been exposed to the potentially deadly disease pilchard orthomyxovirus, (POM-V) into Norfolk Bay, near red handfish habitat, with EPA approval.

Scientists and conservationists were enraged. Yet the threat to the red handfish from both POM-V and the inevitable increased turbidity of water from pollution and activity—a key factor in destroying red handfish habitat—were denied by the salmon industry and Wes Ford, the director of the EPA.

Rachelle Hawkins, head biologist at Seahorse World and a member of the National Handfish Recovery

Team, begged to differ. 'We feel like it's a kick in the guts for the move to be made,' she said, 'to place more risks, pose more threats on the species when such a concerted effort is being made to try and save it.'[245]

The kicks in the gut never stop coming. As scientists had warned about the impacts of the Macquarie Harbour expansion on the maugean skate, so too did they warn about the impacts of the massive Storm Bay expansion by the salmon industry on handfish habitat.[246]

And once again they were ignored.

Unlike real farmers, the salmon corporations don't own the aquatic commons and their wonders, like the red handfish, like the maugean skate, which these corporations destroy in their search for ever-more profit.

The people do.

Not Tassal. Not Huon Aquaculture. Not Petuna.

And not so very long ago, people still revelled in the bounty of those commons and that wonder, and the serenity and beauty, which was theirs too. It was a world loved by and belonging to the Tasmanian people. Until, thirty-five years ago, the first fish farm appeared. And then another, and another, and a soul world of sea and fish and serenity began to vanish.

Meanwhile, in a world that too often felt otherwise, Tasmania had come to stand for an idea of purity and goodness, of harmony and balance. Yet this idea—for it was no more than that—had paradoxically arisen out of half a century of conflict, of the islanders fighting first their government, to save their wild rivers from being dammed, and then a corporation, to stop their great forests from being woodchipped. The salmon industry learnt one essential lesson from that conflict: the idea of purity and goodness was too powerful to fight. Instead, they would exploit it. They would trade on the idea of the wild, pure island; they would cloak their ugly rapacity with the beauty of that idea.

But beyond its seductive clean, green and healthy marketing, beneath its huge floating feedlots, hidden underwater, the salmon industry was destroying everything. Like many, I had failed to see what was apparent. Hiding in the shadows, hidden in the dark, buried underwater, the truth was kept away from us all. But it was there.

The problem, finally, wasn't the industry or the government, but us. It was we Tasmanians, after all, who had believed there were no constraints to what our technology could create, without consequence, from the ocean. It was we who had thought that we could trash our seas, like we had so many other things, and somehow there would be no impact. It was we who had accepted the lie of jobs though the jobs never really came. It was we who believed that the industry made us more prosperous, when everywhere everyone knew someone whose life had been impoverished. It was we who thought the riches our lives once had—the sea, the scallops and oysters and crayfish and abalone and flathead, the seadragons and dolphins; the serenity, the different sound of different birds' wings cutting the air above, a pardalote, a sea eagle—could be traded for a corporate bottom line and that not be a loss for all.

And it was we who stayed silent for too long.

Only too late did it become clear that the promise of a cheap, highly manipulated protein for some at the expense of many had been the wrong bargain to make from the beginning.

What slowly became apparent is that the Tasmanian salmon farmers are engaged in a deadly, pitiless war with nature. And as global heating accelerates, it is a war they can only lose. But what do they care? In the short term they can hold it all at bay, as long as they can continue having the environment and the community pay the ever-increasing costs they are running up.

Because the coastal inshore leases are far cheaper to run and thus more profitable, the industry continues doubling down on antibiotics and the heavy industrialisation of its sites to mitigate the worst effects of climate change on its fish. For as long as the industry can keep a lid on the growing outcry about the mounting environmental cost, stave off proper regulation, and evade paying fair rental on public waters, it can keep making money.

As the arguments in support of the Tasmanian salmon industry are stripped away, the only one that remains is that it produces protein which, if not necessary to the starving masses, and in reality stealing food from them, is still what its Australian middle-class market currently wants: a pink fish-finger for the twenty-first century.

Which is to say the industry makes money. For now.

But those profits may not last.

Other, cleaner technologies are emerging to produce the same protein. In the US, Asia and Europe, companies are rushing to perfect salmon grown in labs from fish stem cells, similar to artificial meat. As these companies scale up and their costs come down, such protein can be expected to disrupt the market, as artificial meat already has. In the US, San Francisco's Wildtype is already producing edible, cell-based artificial salmon, and is now working on manufacturing it at a commercially feasible price.[247] In Europe Danish company Revo has developed technology that uses plant proteins to 3D-print alternative, vegan salmon products, which Revo plans to start selling in mid-2021.[248] All these technologies claim much lower carbon footprints than traditional salmon farming.

While such technologies are in their infancy, land-based systems, in which salmon are grown in giant tanks on land, are fully developed and exploding around the world. These farms presently cost more to produce fish, but their costs are expected to fall as the technology matures.[249] The closed-loop, water-recirculating systems used in land-based farms are extremely water efficient, offering relief from many of the environmental issues that plague marine farmers—from seals and jellyfish through to warm waters, gill amoeba and sea lice; eliminating the need for antibiotics and pesticides; while the wastewater treatment and sludge recycling minimise their environmental footprint.[250] Land-based salmon farms need about an acre of land to produce 1000 tons (907 tonnes), meaning a land farm producing the equivalent of Tasmania's 2019 output of 60,000 tonnes would need fewer than 30 hectares (70 acres) of land.[251]

Using technology developed by multiple Norwegian companies, systems that only a few years ago were experimental, are now big business in Europe, Asia and the US. In Miami, Atlantic Sapphire, a Norwegian company, the share price of which has risen by 280 per cent between 2017 and 2020, is in 2021 midway through building a massive land-based facility, costing US$400 million, which already produces 9000 tonnes of salmon annually and will within ten years produce 220,000 tonnes—nearly quadruple all of Tasmania's annual production.[252]

Land-based salmon farms are even blossoming in the desert. Another Norwegian company, Vikings

Label, announced plans in 2019 to set up a 5000-tonne Atlantic salmon land-based farm in Jeddah in Saudi Arabia; while, a short drive from Dubai in the UAE, a land-based salmon farm backed by the Crown Prince is already in operation.[253] In South Korea, the country's largest fishing company, Dongwon, announced in August 2020 that, using Norwegian company Salmon Evolution's technology, it will create a mega land-based salmon complex at a cost of US$168 million in Gangwon Province to produce 20,000 tonnes of Atlantic salmon. Dongwon's CEO, Lee Myung-woo, was quoted as saying, 'We plan to foster it as Asia's largest fisheries bio-industrial complex in the future.'[254] Four massive projects currently planned in China—long touted as a key future market for Tasmanian salmon—could potentially result in land-based production of 140,000 tonnes, which is more than China's total imports in 2018.[255]

In Norway, the very heartland of Atlantic salmon farming, Sande Aqua's land-based salmon farm will be under construction by the beginning of 2022, and is set to produce 33,000 tonnes, expandable to 66,000 tonnes.[256] Europe's largest land-based salmon farm is to open in Sweden's Sotenäs municipality in 2026, producing a staggering 100,000 tonnes of salmon per year—on a 140 hectare site,[257] while Norwegian salmon tycoon Roger Hofseth has announced plans to build Norway's biggest—and, he claims, the world's cleanest—salmon farm on land in an abandoned mine, also producing 100,000 tonnes of salmon annually, forming, according to *Salmon Business*, 'the world's sixth-largest fish farming group' in the process.[258] Using the thousands of tonnes of resultant sludge that in Tasmania continues to lay waste to marine ecosystems, Hofseth's farm plans to process the salmon faeces into environmentally friendly 'saleable protein', bio-hydrogen and green biogas, providing energy back to the farm, serving to reduce costs and creating additional income streams.[259] The Sotenäs farm is to be powered by 100 per cent green energy, aiming to have zero emissions with a positive carbon footprint, something unachievable with Tasmania's dirty diesel-based aquaculture.[260]

Huon Aquaculture claims a carbon footprint of 2.9 kilograms of carbon dioxide per kilogram of edible product. But the most recent research suggests that this and similar figures are a wild underestimate. In what is the most detailed study to date on the carbon footprint of industrial salmon, a 2020 report by the highly respected Norwegian independent research organisation Sintef found that Norwegian farmed salmon 'caused emissions of between 6.5–8.4 kg CO_2e/kg edible salmon in the market'.[261] This means salmon has double the carbon footprint of chicken (2.9 kilograms of carbon dioxide per kilogram of meat) and more than pork (6.3 kilograms of carbon dioxide) and far, far more than vegetable-based food (between 0.9 and 1.3 kilograms of carbon dioxide).[262] When airfreighted to distant markets, the footprint swells: flying salmon from Norway to Shanghai gave the fish a whopping 19.4 kilogram carbon footprint. Hobart to Shanghai— to where Tasmanian salmon is also exported with an Australian taxpayers' subsidy[263]—is 500 kilometres further than Oslo to Shanghai.

Land-based systems are not perfect—as well as needing proper regulation they are not, of themselves, an answer to the significant problems that the production of fish feed presents. But they do stop the destruction of marine ecosystems and they are able to significantly drive down their carbon footprint in two ways—by using only renewable energy, as Sotenäs will, and because they can be built next to major urban markets rather than having to airfreight their product.

At some point in the next decade, it appears inevitable that a carbon-pricing mechanism will be introduced in Australia. And any such mechanism will significantly increase the price of dirty Tasmanian salmon in comparison to land-based salmon that can be grown using recyclable energy. Ocean-produced salmon risk becoming to land-based salmon what the petrol car is to the electric. And Tasmanian marine salmon farms, with their heavy industrial technology, risk becoming what economists term 'stranded assets'—once valuable infrastructure that can no longer produce income and so becomes worthless.

Labelling the new technology Aquaculture 2.0, the Dutch multinational financial group Rabobank released a major report in late 2019 that concluded that land-based salmon farms are now primed to change fish farming globally, becoming 'a disruptive aquaculture technology within 10 years—not only in terms of adding volumes to salmon production, but also potentially disrupting trade flows, supply chains, and the marketing of salmon'. The report saw 'the tide turning', estimating land-based farms will account for 25 per cent of the global market by 2030, identifying over fifty major land-based projects in China, Russia, Japan, Iceland, Norway, Africa, US, Vietnam and Canada.[264]

'For those in the salmon industry and other aquaculture value-chain operations,' *Salmon Business* declared in 2019, 'now is the time to decide if they should invest in RAS [land based] or invest to ensure they stay ahead of RAS, as this technology matures, grows, and disrupts the market.'[265]

In its 2019 report, Rabobank identified an expected output of 250,000 tonnes of salmon from all proposed land-based sites by 2030. Twelve months later, as if in fulfilment of its predictions of disruption, Rabobank reported that figure had grown sixfold, to a staggering 1.6 million tonnes—or 70 per cent of global salmon production in 2020 if all proposed land-based facilities were to be built.[266]

If it comes to a marketing war between, say, a Sydney or Melbourne land-based salmon producer and a Tasmanian producer, the land-based farmers can claim their products are local, greener and cleaner, more sustainable and more environmentally friendly, while the Tasmanian sea-based producers will have to fall back on the state's brand and the fact their fish come from open waters.

But if those waters are being polluted, if those clean, green values are being trashed by the Tasmanian salmon farmers, if iconic areas such as Bruny Island, and even World Heritage Areas, are being ruined by heavy industrialisation, their marine ecosystems imperilled, endangered species threatened with extinction; if the industry's social licence is clearly revoked by communities who want these companies gone from their waters; if there is a possibility of heavy-metal contamination of beloved coastlines and celebrated wild seafood, why on earth would anyone want to swallow such a slimy product?

And if the Tasmanian regulators continue to apply no meaningful standards when it comes to these matters, or the associated issues of animal welfare;

if they enable the salmon industry's worst practices rather than effectively regulating them; if the Tasmanian government routinely excuses the industry's failings rather than investigating them; and if the Tasmanian government is so wilfully ignorant or reckless that it can only endorse and promote the wildest claims of rogue salmon corporations, how can anyone feel safe eating Tasmanian salmon?

Tasmanian salmon farmers are well aware that land-based farming is coming and coming quickly. According to one senior bureaucrat, whenever new environmental regulations are mooted, Tassal threatens Tasmanian politicians with moving their entire operation to land-based facilities on mainland Australia. Though they don't say so loudly, they are already preparing for the inevitable. Huon's land-based Whale Point facility, in Huon's own words, 'allows us to continue to gain experience in this new [land-based] technology which will positively shape the way we farm in the future'.[267] Tassal's Hamilton hatchery serves a similar purpose, extending the growth period of smolt.[268]

According to Huon, 'The commercial reality is that . . . on shore facilities will be built next door to the customer base to lower other overheads such as freight etc. So rather than salmon being grown in Tasmania and creating jobs and opportunity they will be grown in Sydney, China or Asia.'[269]

One Tasmanian company, the smallest, Petuna, may well be the first to make the leap into full-scale land-based salmon production. Petuna was purchased in January 2020 by New Zealand company Sealord, which is half-owned by Japanese seafood giant Nissui. Three months later Nissui, with fellow Japanese giant Marubeni, jointly purchased a 66.7 per cent stake in Danish Salmon, a leader in land-based salmon farming, with the aim of growing its business in Europe and expanding its land-based operation 'to countries outside of Europe as well', citing land-based farming's 'potential to minimise environmental impact by reducing . . . the risk of water pollution'.[270]

If the Tasmanian salmon industry is effectively already admitting it's a dinosaur, you would think that the state government would be doing all it could to facilitate a timely transition that would advantage Tasmania and safeguard jobs, moving to land-based salmon farming but trying to do it locally, using the Tasmanian brand and establishing itself as the national leader in the new technology.

But it is not.

Rather than seeking to seriously regulate an industry already working well beyond its ecological limits; instead of acting to ensure a transition takes place in an orderly, planned way, an utterly irresponsible Tasmanian government is supporting the industry in a spiralling dependency on some of its worst practices, as it doubles down on the heavy industrialisation of coastal inshore sites.

And so inevitably—in the next decade or two, but most likely sooner—new companies will set up land-based salmon farms in Melbourne and Sydney, using Norwegian technology that offers cleaner, greener salmon; and the Tasmanian salmon industry will become a white elephant.

If the future of Tasmanian salmon farming is to be as it presently operates, it's a grim, grubby and dispiriting prospect—and for what? At the end—whenever that is, five or fifteen years, but not that far away—the industry will become land-based and the state's salmon industry will collapse. Jobs will be lost and the environment it trashed will be gone, perhaps forever.

Until that moment the lie will continue, sustained by marketing campaigns and the rhetoric of politicians too lazy or too compromised to speak the truth. Beyond the island's ruined shores will remain heart-tugging images of young women holding silvery salmons and bearded men in beanies grinning, all of it endorsed by some rentable greenwashing conservation group.

But come to Tasmania. Talk to the abalone diver, the resident, the shackie, the professional fisherman, the recreational fisherman, the yachtie, the kayaker, the diver, the surfie and the scientist. Talk to the public servant whose job has been imperilled, the business-people who have had their livelihoods threatened, the farmer who has been sold out and bought up, the scientist who no longer has work in Tasmania. Talk to the locals, who have returned generation after generation to the same piece of coastline because it's their soul country. Talk to them about the aching sadness.

As Gerard Castles says, 'It's our Tasmania—not Tassal's.'

Are we more interested in how the slickly presented terracotta fillet plates up than the destruction that manufactured it? Are we so taken with the whis-ky-cured salmon gravlax, the salmon pate, the salmon bacon, the cutlet, that we can't be bothered with listening, looking, thinking of how a fish that cannot live in our waters lives in our waters? To wonder how something seemingly so natural might just be tech-nologically contrived? To ponder whether that salmon in its heat-shrunk plastic casing is a fish or a lie?

To ask one simple question: what are we *eating* when we eat Tasmanian salmon?

For we eat horror: factory-farmed chicken heads and guts and claws and feathers, as well as petrochemi-cal dyes, possible carcinogens and antibiotic residue. We dine on destruction: idyllic worlds reduced to industrial complexes that toil to the thud of dirty diesels day and night keeping millions of tortured fish alive with chemicals and dubious feed products; we sup on people's lives destroyed by noise and official contempt. And we are eating the silencing by anonymous threats, pay-offs and the use of confidentiality and non-disclosure agreements of anyone with an opinion contrary to that of the salmon industry.

And that's just the people.

We are also eating the near-destruction of one marine species, the maugean skate, and the possible destruction of another, the red handfish—to say nothing of the lifelong suffering of millions of caged salmon. We are eating the slow poisoning of Hobart's drinking water. The destruction of Macquarie Harbour. The growing sickness of the once-glorious D'Entrecasteaux Channel. We are eating algal blooms and writhing white worms spreading out from salmon-cage death zones into World Heritage Areas; we are swilling sludge, the equivalent of ten times Tasmania's sewage effluent pouring into the wild beauty of Storm Bay. We are eating floating debris littering once pristine beaches and threatening boaters' lives. Microplastic pollution that may be entering the food chains of recreational and commercial fisheries. We are dining off metre-high piles of fish faeces, churning heavy metals in a recreational fishery—the same waters off Bruny Island where rich tourists are routinely taken on gourmet boat tours sampling wild seafood. We are eating vanishing penguins, vanishing dolphins, choking on the vanishing maireeners, the vanishing flathead, the dead seals. We are devouring a beautiful world sacred to many Tasmanians that has been reduced to a quarry for the greed of a few.

Healthy? Clean and green? Wild?

9

LATE ON OUR VERY FIRST DAY AT OUR SHACK all those years ago, we walked as a family along the rocky foreshore of North Bruny Island, making our way to an isolated beach. At the sandstone point that marked one end of the beach's bay, we stopped, struck silent, as there crawled out from the sea and onto the oyster-encrusted, seaweed-festooned rock the most marvellous creature: an octopus.

We were perhaps five metres away, but the octopus seemed unperturbed. There was, I remember—and I don't know why I remember this detail—a slight onshore wind that ruffled the water. It was the magical inter-tidal time between day and night, when the Tasmanian light is deeply rich in saturated inky reds and iron-blues. The distant mountain range spread its deep shadow.

The octopus sat up, head upright, surveying its world, the gathering dusk, and its slick body, like its movements, seemed to slide from colour to colour. Our children, small, the twins no more than toddlers, Majda's father, Majda, me: we all watched.

Its movements, which were so fluid and could be both rapid and languid, were like water itself, as if the animal was no more or less than the sea summoned into shape and being.

I first wrote, 'It was as if it were some magical blessing being bestowed,' but that's a crude shorthand that misrepresents more than it reveals. We felt, I think, that on this island, which in those years was regarded as a commonplace sort of world, was the magical kingdom of many things, of which we were simply one more. And in that universe, we felt alive and happy and somehow understood—and we understood our place within its realm, a part no more but no less.

I don't recall what happened next: at some point, though, the animal's many legs began undulating and as if it were rain or a dying wave, it merged back into the waters of the Channel.

Sometimes of a night, if there were no winds and the Channel was calm, we would perilously load up our twelve-foot tinny with our kids and others— cousins, friends—and in the darkness, trailing an old flounder light in the water, row along the shallow reefs that ran beside the coastline, spotting striped cowfish, wrasse, squid, octopus, seahorses and seadragons.

Commonplace sea creatures, but for us miraculous and gorgeous in their luminous colours, their liquid movements. *The immense wonder.* It was a world of astonishments, a world of dreams. When I was there ideas and thoughts that were laboured, heavy things, grew fins and wings, became other, alive, strange even to me, and all I could do was follow them into the seaweed to become people, stories, books. They helped me write my stories. I write this in the hope that I might now help them.

Endnotes

1 James Hall with Stephen Wisenthal, 'Tassal Group Gobbles Up Aquatas', *Australian Financial Review*, 18 March 2005, afr.com/politics/ tassal-group-gobbles-up-aquatas-20050318-jl6sw

2 Tony Briscoe, 'The rise and rise of Tasmania's Atlantic salmon industry, from zero to a billion dollars in three decades', ABC News, 1 December 2020, abc.net.au/news/rural/2020-12-01/ tasmanian-atlantic-salmon-industry-growth-over-30-years/12923592

3 Department of Primary Industries, Parks, Water and Environment (DPIPWE), 'Sustainable industry growth plan for the salmon industry', Tasmanian Government, December 2017, p. 2, dpipwe.tas.gov.au/ Documents/Salmon%20Plan%20-%20One%20Year%20Review.pdf

4 In a public submission last year, TasWater wrote that it was 'about to embark on a $200 million upgrade to its Bryn Estyn Water Treatment Plant, in part due to the need to manage taste and odour problems associated with algal growth in the Derwent River,' By 2021 the cost had blown out to $240 million, according to answers made by TasWater in reply to questions put by the author in February 2021. TasWater, Submission No. 38, Rural Water Use Strategy Position Paper—Submissions Received, 2020, p. 185, dpipwe.tas. gov.au/Documents/RWUS%20Position%20Paper_Submissions%20 Received.pdf

5 Australia Institute, Submission to the Legislative Council Fin Fish Farming in Tasmania Inquiry, 28 November 2019, p. 16, parliament.

tas.gov.au/ctee/Council/Submissions/FIN%20FISH/Submissions%20
1%20-%20125/69%20Australia%20Institute.pdf

6   'Mercury and Health', World Health Organization, 2017, who.int/en/
     news-room/fact-sheets/detail/mercury-and-health

7   Editorial, 'Banging our heads at the heavy metal', *Mercury*, 21 December
     2016, themercury.com.au/news/opinion/editorial-banging-our-heads-
     at-the-heavy-metal/news-story/b44874d872b62f9a95d97d8a81fcd947

8   C. Coughanowr, et al., 'State of the Derwent Estuary: a review of
     environmental data from 2009 to 2014', 2015, see chapters 7, 8 and 10
     in particular, derwentestuary.org.au/assets/State_of_the_Derwent_
     Estuary_2015.pdf

9   J. Banks, and J. Ross, 'From sink to source: how changing oxygen
     conditions can remobilise heavy metals from contaminated sedi-
     ments,' report prepared by TAFI for Derwent Estuary Program Water
     Quality Improvement Plan, 2009.

10   The Marine Farming Planning Review Panel 'is a statutory body estab-
     lished under the Marine Farming Planning Act (1995) . . . to consider
     marine farming planning matters and make recommendations to the
     Minister. The Panel comprises up to nine individuals appointed by the
     Governor.' DPIPWE, Submission to the Legislative Council Fin Fish
     Farming in Tasmania Inquiry, 4 December 2019, p. 10, parliament.
     tas.gov.au/ctee/Council/Submissions/FIN%20FISH/Submissions%20
     126%20-%20223/221%20DPIPWE.pdf

11   Colin Buxton & Assoc., letter responding to statements, Submission
     92, 'An Inquiry into the Regulation of the Fin-Fish Aquaculture
     Industry in Tasmania,' Senate, Commonwealth of Australia, 2015, aph.
     gov.au/Parliamentary_Business/Committees/Senate/Environment_
     and_Communications/Fin-Fish/Submissions?main_0_content_1_
     RadGrid1ChangePage=5_20

12   Annah Fromberg, 'New ship fight looms in Tasmania over factory
     trawler Geelong Star', ABC News, 13 April 2015, abc.net.au/
     news/2015-04-13/new-ship-fight-looms-over-factory-trawler-geelong
     -star/638996

13   Laura Kelly, 'The Science on Salmon Farming Tells a Much More
     Nuanced Tale', *Mercury*, 23 February 2017, themercury.com.au/news/

opinion/talking-point-the-science-on-salmon-farming-tells-a-much-more-nuanced-tale/news-story/49f4ed6f558e9bdfd0028aacccb4f3fc

14 Tasmanian Conservation Trust, Submission 92, 'An Inquiry into the Regulation of the Fin-Fish Aquaculture Industry in Tasmania,' op cit.

15 Jess Feehely and Tom Baxter, 'Tasmania. Changes to Marine Farming Legislation', *National Environment Law Review,* 2011, p. 22, austlii.edu.au/au/journals/NatEnvLawRw/2011/63.pdf

16 Barbara Nowak and Louise Cherrie, Submission to the Legislative Council Fin Fish Farming in Tasmania Inquiry, 29 November 2019, parliament.tas.gov.au/ctee/Council/Submissions/FIN%20FISH/Submissions%201%20-%20125/51%20Barbara%20Nowak_Redacted.pdf

17 Louise Cherrie, Submission to the Legislative Council Fin Fish Farming in Tasmania Inquiry, 29 November 2019, parliament.tas.gov.au/ctee/Council/Submissions/FIN%20FISH/Submissions%201%20-%20125/55%20Louise%20Cherrie.pdf

18 Cherrie, Submission, op cit.; Nowak and Cherrie, Submission, op cit.

19 Nowak and Cherrie, Submission, op cit.

20 Jamie Kirkpatrick et al., 'The Reverse Precautionary Principle: Science, The Environment and the Salmon Aquaculture Industry in Macquarie Harbour, Tasmania, Australia', CSIRO Publishing, 12 September 2017, p. 29, publish.csiro.au/PC/PC17014. This article deserves a far wider audience than its paywalled home permits, not only for its incisive study of what happened at Macquarie Harbour, but also for its denunciation of political, regulatory and scientific dissembling and its consequences, and its discussion on the growth of corporate- and industry-sponsored science at the expense of public science, and the many necessary questions which are, in consequence, never asked.

21 Australian Greens Dissenting Report, 'Inquiry into the Regulation of the Fin-Fish Aquaculture Industry in Tasmania', aph.gov.au/Parliamentary_Business/Committees/Senate/Environment_and_Communications/Fin-Fish/Report/d02

22 Siobhan Galea, Emily Street and James Dunlevie, 'Macquarie Harbour salmon: 1.35 million fish deaths prompt call to "empty" waterway of farms', ABC News, 29 May 2018, abc.net.au/news/2018-05-29/salmon-deaths-in-macquarie-harbour-top-one-million-epa-says/9810720

23 Jamie Kirkpatrick et al., op cit., p. 30

24 'Environment watchdog orders Tassal to destock salmon lease in Macquarie Harbour', ABC News, 9 February 2019, abc.net.au/ news/2017-02-08/tassal-told-to-destock-salmon-pens-macquarie -harbour/8250394

25 Marine Life Network, 'Maugean Skate', marinelife.org.au/?page_ id=940

26 Jamie Kirkpatrick et al., op cit., p. 32.

27 Ibid.

28 Cherrie, Submission, op cit.

29 Alexandra Humphries, 'Questions over approval of Storm Bay salmon farming', ABC News, 31 January 2020, abc.net.au/news/2021-01-31/ storm-bay-salmon-furore/13103154

30 Alexandra Humphries, 'Experts' scathing comments about "independent" Tasmanian fish farm review panel revealed', ABC News, 3 November 2020, abc.net.au/news/2020-11-03/scathing-comments-about-fish-farm-review-panel-revealed/12840010

31 Barbara Nowak and Louise Cherrie, Submission, 29 November 2019, op cit.

32 Alexandra Humphries, op cit.

33 'There is only one Tasmanian feed producer, Gibson's . . . Gibson's imports substantial quantities of fish meal for its fish feed pellet production', Productivity Commission report, 'Australian Atlantic Salmon: Effects of Import Competition', 20 December 1996, p. 9, pc.gov.au/research/supporting/salmon/salmon.pdf

Announcing a federal government project to research alternatives in salmon feed in 1998, the then minister for Resources and Energy, Warwick Parer, said, 'The industry currently uses feeds based on imported fishmeal, such as Peruvian anchovies', Senator Warwick Parer, Minister for Resources and Energy, 'Australian Food for Australian Salmon', media release, 6 August 1998, parlinfo.aph.gov. au/parlInfo/search/display/display.w3p;query=Id%3A%22media%2F-pressrel%2F55805%22;src1=sm1

'Anchovy meal . . . is the main source of protein in Atlantic salmon feeds', Chris Carter et al., 'Aquaculture Feed Development for Atlantic

Salmon, University of Tasmanian and FRDC, 2002, pp. 10, 13, frdc. com.au/Archived-Reports/FRDC%20Projects/1998-322-DLD.pdf

34 'The fish you don't know you eat', Global Reporting Program in partnership with NBC News, British Columbia's Graduate School of Journalism (undated), globalreportingprogram.org/fishmeal

35 Andrew Wasley, 'One thing I've learned about modern farming – we shouldn't do it like this', *Guardian*, 4 August 2020, theguardian.com/ environment/2020/aug/04/one-thing-ive-learned-about-modern-farming-we-shouldnt-do-it-like-this

36 Ibid.

37 Tassal, 'What do we feed our salmon', factsheet, Tassal website, p. 4, tassal.com.au/wp-content/uploads/2014/11/fact-sheet-1.pdf

38 Tim Cushion et al., 'Most fish destined for fishmeal production are food-grade fish', *Fish and Fisheries*, 13 February 2017, abstract, onlinelibrary.wiley.com/doi/full/10.1111/faf.12209

39 Changing Markets Foundation, 'Fishing for Catastrophe: How global aquaculture supply chains are leading to the destruction of wild fish stocks and depriving people of food in India, Vietnam and The Gambia', October 2019, pp. 28, 69, changingmarkets.org/ wp-content/uploads/2019/10/CM-WEB-FINAL-FISHING-FOR-CATASTROPHE-2019.pdf

40 Rob Fletcher, 'Fresh furore over use of fishmeal and fish oil in aquafeeds', *The Fish Site*, 15 October 2019, thefishsite.com/articles/ fresh-furore-over-use-of-fishmeal-and-fish-oil-in-aquafeeds

41 Changing Markets Foundation, op cit., pp. 6, 66 ff.

42 'The fish you don't know you eat', Global Reporting Program, op cit.

43 Ibid.

44 US Environment Protection Agency, 'R.E.D. Facts', November 2004, p. 2, archive.epa.gov/pesticides/reregistration/web/pdf/0003fact.pdf

45 Louise Harkell, 'Aquaculture sector mulls impact of potential EU ban on ethoxyquin', 29 August 2019, *Undercurrent News*, undercurrentnews.com/2019/08/19/aquaculture-sector-mulls-impact -of-potential-eu-ban-on-ethoxyquin/

46 IFFO, 'Antioxidants and Fishmeal', IFFO website, iffo.com/ antioxidants-and-fishmeal

47 Elena Blaszczyk et al., 'Ethoxyquin: An Antioxidant Used in Animal Feed', *International Journal of Food Science*, 30 April 2013, ncbi.nlm.nih. gov/pmc/articles/PMC4745505/

48 Ibid.

49 'Ethoxyquin: safety still not sufficiently proven', *Eurofish*, undated, eurofishmagazine.com/sections/aquaculture/item/131-safety-still-not -sufficiently-proven

50 Elena Blaszczyk et al., op cit.

51 Sylvain Merel et al., 'Identification of Ethoxyquin and its transformation products in salmon after controlled dietary exposure via fish feed', *Food Chemistry*, March 2019, p. 262, researchgate.net/publication/331692213_ Identification_of_ethoxyquin_and_its_transformation_products _in_salmon_after_controlled_dietary_exposure_via_fish_feed

52 Simen Saetre, Kjetil Ostli, 'What we do not know about salmon', *Morgenbladet*, 5 April 2018, morgenbladet.no/aktuelt/2018/04/det-vi -ikke-vet-om-laksen

53 Ibid.

54 Australia New Zealand Food Standards Code, 'Schedule 15 – Substances that may be used as food additives', Federal Register of Legislation, Australian Government, 20 March 2020, legislation.gov. au/Series/F2015L00439

55 Marc H. G. Berntssen et al., 'Chemical contaminants in aquafeeds and Atlantic salmon (Salmo salar) following the use of traditional versus alternative feed ingredients', *Chemosphere*, January 2010, pubmed. ncbi.nlm.nih.gov/20045551/

56 'Animal Proteins Standards,' Australian Renderers Association and Stockfeed Manufacturers Association of Australia, 1 August 2015, p. 13, graintrade.org.au/sites/default/files/file/Commodity%20Standards/ 2015_2016/Section%2007%20-%20Animal%20Proteins%20201516.pdf

57 'Foreign Matter Contamination of Rendering Raw Material', Australian Renderers Association, 17 May 2016, mintrac.com.au/docs/ pdf/20170921_Foreign_Matter_Contamination.pdf

58 Torgeir P. Krokfjord, 'Revealing report hits like a bomb at Norway's aquaculture giants: This is completely unacceptable', *Dagbladet*, 20 October 2018, dagbladet.no/nyheter/avslorende-rapport-slar-ned

-som-bombe-hos-norges-oppdrettsgiganter---dette-er-helt-uaksept abelt/70363486

59 Skretting Sustainability Report 2018, skretting.com/en/sustainability/ reports/sustainability-report-2018/ingredients/what-is-a-responsible -soy-supply-chain/

60 'Integrated Sustainability Report 2019', BioMar website, p. 76, biomar. com/globalassets/.global/pdf-files/reports/biomar-sustainability-report-2019.pdf

61 Heidi Lundeberg et al., 'From Brazilian farms to Norwegian Tables. A Report about soya in Norwegian salmon farms', Rainforest Foundation, 2017, p. 4, d5i6isoeze552.cloudfront.net/documents/Publikasjoner/ Andre-rapporter/Rapport_Soya_eng.pdf

62 Jillian Fry et al., 'Environmental health impacts of feeding crops to farmed fish', *Environment International*, 11 March 2016, pp. 204, 210, sciencedirect.com/science/article/pii/S0160412016300587

63 Rachel Mutter, 'Greig Seafood: "Lack of adequate action" by soy buyers increases risk for entire salmon farming industry', *Intrafish*, 16 December 2020, intrafish.com/feed/grieg-seafood-lack-of-adequate-action-by-soy-buyers-increases-risk-for-entire-salmon-farming -industry/2-1-931778

64 Retno Kusumaningtyas et al., 'Setting the bar for deforestation-free soy in Europe. A Benchmark to assess the sustainability of voluntary standard systems', Profundo, March 2019, https://www.iscc-system. org/wp-content/uploads/2019/03/Deforestation-Free-Benchmark-of-FEFAC-Compliant-Standard-190312.pdf

65 Heidi Lundeberg et al., op cit., pp. 25 and 31

66 Ibid., p. 31

67 'Skretting Sustainability Report 2018', p. 30, Skretting website, https://www.skretting.com/siteassets/global/sustainability/skretting-sustainability-report-16-july.pdf?v=4aef61

68 Ibid.

69 'Skretting Sustainability Report, 2019', 14.3, Skretting website, skretting.com/en-au/sustainability/sustainability-reporting/ sustainability-report-2019/14.-responsible-sourcing/14.3-the-origin-of-soy-ingredients/

70　BioMar Sourcing Policy, April 2015, biomar.com/globalassets/.global/pdf-files/biomar-sourcing-policy.pdf

71　Uki Goni, 'Soy destruction in Argentina leads straight to our dinner plates', Guardian, 26 October 2018, theguardian.com/environment/2018/oct/26/soy-destruction-deforestation-in-argentina-leads-straight-to-our-dinner-plates

72　Jane Byrne, 'BioMar shows its soy suppliers are legally compliant', FeedNavigator, 15 April 2019, feednavigator.com/Article/2019/04/15/BioMar-probe-shows-its-soy-suppliers-are-legally-compliant

73　Rachel Mutter, op cit.

74　Alan Barrett et al., 'Long Term World Soybean Outlook', Ussoy.org, 21 November 2019, ussoy.org/long-term-world-soybean-outlook/ 'Fish farming executives make a lame attempt to solve their big deforestation problem', Grain, 5 March 2020, grain.org/en/article/6425-fish-farming-corporations-make-a-lame-attempt-to-solve-their-big-deforestation-problem

75　Jean Do Kin, 'Aller Aqua eliminates South American soya in feed', Hatchery International, 4 February 2021, hatcheryinternational.com/aller-aqua-eliminates-south-american-soya-in-feed/

76　Peter Nichols, 'Readily Available Sources of Long-Chain Omega-3 Oils: Is Farmed Australian Seafood a Better Source of the Good Oil than Wild-Caught Seafood?', Nutrients, 11 March 2014, mdpi.com/2072-6643/6/3/1063

77　M. Sprague et al., 'Impact of sustainable feeds on omega-3 long-chain fatty acid levels in farmed Atlantic salmon, 2006–2015', Nature, 22 February 2016, nature.com/articles/srep21892

78　Lisa Duchene, 'Omega-6s and the threat to seafood's healthy halo', Global Aquaculture Alliance, 20 January 2017, aquaculturealliance.org/advocate/omega-6s-and-the-threat-to-seafoods-healthy-halo/

79　Nini Sissener, 'Correction: Are we what we eat? Changes to the feed fatty acid composition of farmed salmon and its effects through the food chain', Journal of Experimental Biologists, 2018, jeb.biologists.org/content/jexbio/221/Suppl_1/jeb161521.full.pdf

80　Lisa Duchene, op cit.

81　Huon Aquaculture, 'How to Be an Ethical Consumer', Huon

Aquaculture website, huonaqua.com.au/huon-hub/how-to-be-an-ethical-consumer/

82 Amelia White, 'A Comprehensive Analysis of Efficiency in the Tasmanian Salmon Industry', PhD, Bond University, 2013, p. 26, pure.bond.edu.au/ws/portalfiles/portal/36347633/Amelia_White_Thesis.pdf

83 Tassal CEO Mark Ryan summed up this argument in his letter introducing Tassal's submission to the Tasmanian Legislative Council's Inquiry into Fin Fish Farming in this way: 'Globally, with increasing pressures on our planet, access to arable land restrictive and wild fisheries plateauing from protecting vulnerable stocks, a key aspect to the future of the world's food supply is aquaculture. Our industry is a solution to addressing increased demand for a more sustainable, nutritious and efficient sources of protein.' Tassal, Submission to the Legislative Council Fin Fish Farming in Tasmania Inquiry, 29 November 2019, tassalgroup.com.au/wp-content/uploads/sites/2/2020/01/TASSAL-GROUP-_-INQUIRY-SUBMISSION-29.11.19-.pdf

84 Allison Guy, 'Dying Salmon Pink for Farms and Profit', *Next Nature*, 20 June 2012, nextnature.net/story/2012/dyeing-salmon-pink-for-farms-and-profit
'The SalmoFan color measurement tools' DSM website, dsm.com/markets/anh/en_US/products/products-solutions/products_solutions_tools/Products_solutions_tools_salmon.html

85 Nick Clark, 'Feed supplier sues Huon Aquaculture, *Mercury*, 13 January 2019

86 'Tassal announces move to natural salmon feed pigment, denies move prompted by *Four Corners*', ABC News, 2 November 2016, abc.net.au/news/2016-11-03/tassal-move-to-natural-astaxanthin-not-due-to-4corners-big-fish/7992972

87 20 per cent cost—Chris Loew, 'Salmon a hit health food in Japan', *Seafood Source*, 2 December 2012, seafoodsource.com/news/food-safety-health/salmon-a-hit-health-food-in-japan.
Prices of astaxanthin—Samuel Jannel et al., 'Novel Insights into the Biotechnological Production of *Haematococcus pluvalis*-Derived Astaxanthin', *Journal of Marine Science and Engineering*, 10 October 2020, https://www.mdpi.com/2077-1312/8/10/789

88 Huon Aquaculture, Submission to the Legislative Council Fin Fish Farming in Tasmania Inquiry, November 2019, p. 47, parliament.tas. gov.au/ctee/council/Submissions/FIN%20FISH/Submissions%201%20 -%20125/87%20Huon%20Aquaculture%20Company%20Pty%20Ltd.pdf

89 Tassal, 'Our Salmon', Tassal website, tassalgroup.com.au/our-product /our-salmon/

90 Tassal, 'Anti Ageing', Tassal website, purebeautyfood.com/anti-ageing.html

91 Bob Capelli et al., 'Synthetic astaxanthin is significantly inferior to algal-based astaxanthin as an antioxidant and may not be suitable as a human nutraceutical supplement', *Nutrafoods*, December 2013, researchgate. net/publication/263169974_Synthetic_astaxanthin_is_significantly_ inferior_to_algal-based_astaxanthin_as_an_antioxidant_and_may _not_be_suitable_as_a_human_nutraceutical_supplement

92 Ibid.

93 Ibid.

94 Jannel et al., op cit., p. 2

95 Huon Aquaculture, 'Heart, Brain and Skin', Huon Aquaculture website, huonaqua.com.au/health/heart-brain-skin/

96 Huon Aquaculture, 'Astaxanthin', Huon Aquaculture website, July 2020, huonaqua.com.au/wp-content/uploads/2020/09/Astaxanthin-Fact-Sheet-FINAL.pdf

97 Ibid.

98 'Can you say Asta-zan-thin?' *Nutrition News*, 2006 special edition, cyanotech.com/pdfs/bioastin/batl61.pdf

99 Charles Benbrook, 'Antibiotic Drug Use in US Aquaculture', IATP report, February 2002, p. 4, studylib.net/doc/7729836/antibiotic-drug -use-in-us-aquaculture

100 Claudio D. Miranda et al., 'Bacterial resistance to oxytetracycline in Chilean salmon farming', *Aquaculture*, 23 September 2002, sciencedirect.com/science/article/abs/pii/S0044848602001242

101 'Study: Farmed Fish Could Be Another Source of Antibiotic Resistance', Food Safety News, 28 October 2014, foodsafetynews.com/2014/ 10/farmed-fish-could-be-another-source-of-antibiotic-resistance

102 Ole E. Heuer et al., 'Human Health Consequences of Use of

Antimicrobial Agents in Aquaculture', *Clinical Infectious Diseases*, 15 October 2009, academic.oup.com/cid/article/49/8/1248/428193

103 Christian Molinari, 'Salmon Chile head tapped to improve Chile's relations with Russia', *Seafood Source*, 20 July 2020, seafoodsource.com/news/business-finance/salmonchile-head-tapped-to-improve-chile-s-relations-with-russia

104 WHO, 'Stop Using Antibiotics in Healthy Animals', World Health Organization, 7 November 2017, who.int/news-room/detail/07-11-2017-stop-using-antibiotics-in-healthy-animals-to-prevent-the-spread-of-antibiotic-resistance

105 'Antibiotic Use', Huon Aquaculture website, huonaqua.com.au/our-approach/our-operations/fish-health-welfare-and-biosecurity/antibiotic-use/

106 Esther Han, 'Antibiotics in salmon: Tassal quadruples amount, rivals reduce or eliminate use', *Sydney Morning Herald*, 2 August 2017, smh.com.au/healthcare/antibiotics-in-salmon-tassal-quadruples-amount-rivals-reduce-or-eliminate-use-20170731-gxm5ms.htmln

107 Sustainability Report, 'Antibiotic use at Tassal Australia', Global Salmon Initiative, globalsalmoninitiative.org/en/sustainability-report/sustainability-indicators/

108 Claudio Miranda et al., 'Current Status of the Use of Antibiotics and the Antimicrobial Resistance in the Chilean Salmon Farms', *Frontiers in Microbiology*, 18 June 2018, frontiersin.org/articles/10.3389/fmicb.2018.01284/full

109 Joan Casey et al., 'Industrial Food Animal Production and Community Health', *Current Environment Health Reports*, 5 July 2015, researchgate.net/publication/279861677_Industrial_Food_Animal_Production_and_Community_Health

110 Ferris Jabr, 'It's Official: Fish Feel Pain', *Smithsonian Magazine*, 8 January 2018, smithsonianmag.com/science-nature/fish-feel-pain-180967764/

111 Claudio Miranda et al., op cit.

112 Natalie Whiting, 'Salmon giant Tassal plays down mass death of fish at Okehampton Bay, blames "human error"', ABC News, 8 January 2018, abc.net.au/news/2018-01-08/tassal-plays-down-death-of-30k-salmon-at-okehampton-bay-farm/9310706

113　Marco Vindas et al., 'Brain serotonergic activation in growth-stunted farmed salmon: adaption versus pathology', *Royal Society Open Science*, 1 May 2016, royalsocietypublishing.org/doi/full/10.1098/rsos.160030

114　F. A. Huntingford, C. Adams, 'Behavioural syndromes in farmed fish: implications for production and welfare', *Behaviour*, 1207–1221, 2005, quoted in Vindas et al., op cit.

115　Vindas et al., op cit.

116　A shocking image comparing a growth-stunted salmon and a healthy salmon from a Norwegian salmon farm can be found in Vindas et al., op cit., Figure 1, (2.1 Experimental animals and facilities)

117　Nerissa Hannink, 'Farmed Salmon Hard of Hearing', *Science Matters*, 28 April 2016, pursuit.unimelb.edu.au/articles/farmed-salmon-hard -of-hearing

118　'How are salmon farmed in Australia', RSPCA knowledgebase, 24 November 2020, kb.rspca.org.au/knowledge-base/how-are-salmon -farmed-in-australia/

119　Thomas W. K. Fraser, 'Welfare Considerations of Triploid Fish', *Fisheries Science*, Taylor & Francis online, 20 August 2012, tandfonline. com/doi/abs/10.1080/10641262.2012.704598
Thomas W. K. Fraser, 'Vertebral deformities in interspecific diploid and triploid salmonid hybrids', *Journal of Fish Biology*, 20 April 2020, onlinelibrary.wiley.com/doi/full/10.1111/jfb.14353

120　Nerissa Hannink, op cit.

121　Keri Cronin, 'Ruth Harrison', *Unbound Project*, 24 August 2017, unboundproject.org/ruth-harrison/. See also Carol McKenna, 'Ruth Harrison', *Guardian*, 6 July 2000, theguardian.com/news/2000/jul/06/ guardianobituaries

122　Melissa Eichler, 'The Five Freedoms: A History Lesson', Michigan State University, 6 September 2019, canr.msu.edu/news/an_animal _welfare_history_lesson_on_the_five_freedoms

123　'What are the Five Freedoms of animal welfare?', RSPCA knowledge-base, updated 8 October 2019, kb.rspca.org.au/knowledge-base/ what-are-the-five-freedoms-of-animal-welfare/

124　'Australia's Only RSPCA Approved Salmon', Huon Aquaculture website, huonaqua.com.au/australias-only-rspca-approved-salmon

125 'responsibly sourced'—Richard Baines and Harriet Aird, 'WWF email reveals concern on salmon industry's "negative impact on environment"', ABC News, 11 May 2017, abc.net.au/news/2017-05-11/ wwf-concern-over-salmon-industry-revealed-in-email/8517230; 'ASX documents'—Monika Maedler, Tassal Company Secretary to the Manager Listings, ASX Market Announcements, 24 October 2016, p. 3, asx.com.au/asxpdf/20161024/pdf/43c7b3pzv99j7x.pdf; 'mislead consumers'—Paul Bleakley, 'Big Fish, Small Pond: NGO–Corporate Partnerships and Corruption of the Environmental Certification Process in Tasmanian Aquaculture', *Critical Criminology*, 20 June 2019, abstract, https://link.springer.com/article/10.1007/s10612-019 -09454-8

126 Mark Macaskill, 'RSPCA paid over £500,000 to back Scottish salmon industry', *Sunday Times* (UK), 9 February 2020, thetimes.co.uk/ article/rspca-paid-over-500-000-to-back-scottish-salmon-industry-bqcn7gs22

127 Chris Packham and Megan McCubbin, *Back to Nature: How to love life—and save it*, Hachette, London, 2020, p. 152

128 'Farmed Atlantic Salmon', RSPCA Australia, May 2020, pp. 14, 23, rspcaapproved.org.au/wp-content/uploads/2020/05/2020-05_ FARMEDATLANTICSALMON_Standard.pdf

129 'Triploids versus diploids', Huon Aquaculture factsheet, December 2019, huonaqua.com.au/wp-content/uploads/2020/01/Triploids-Fact-Sheet.pdf

130 'Our operations: Fish health, welfare and biosecurity', Huon Aquaculture website, huonaqua.com.au/our-approach/our-operations/

131 'The Dawn of the New Decade: Annual Report 2020', Huon Aquaculture annual report, p. 10, investors.huonaqua.com.au/ FormBuilder/_Resource/_module/y8hXOlgfxoa4WjSUgjZk7A/docs/ Reports/Annual/HUON_Annual_Report_FY2020.pdf

132 AAP, 'Jellyfish sting Huon Aquaculture's profit', Nine Finance, 29 August 2019, finance.nine.com.au/business-news/huon-aquaculture -s-fy-profit-down-64/33126c79-b875-4afd-b87f-caf88011ee69

133 Lisa-ann Gershwin, *Stung! On jellyfish blooms and the future of the ocean*, University of Chicago Press, Chicago, 2013; Tim Flannery, 'They're

taking over!', *New York Review of Books*, 26 September 2013, nybooks.com/articles/2013/09/26/jellyfish-theyre-taking-over/

134 Lisa-ann Gershwin, 'Positive Feedback Loop Between Jellyfish and Salmon Farming', Submission to the Legislative Council Fin Fish Farming in Tasmania Inquiry, 28 November 2018, p. 3, parliament.tas.gov.au/ctee/Council/Submissions/FIN%20FISH/Submissions%201%20-%20125/40%20Dr%20Lisa-ann%20Gershwin_Redacted.pdf

135 Ibid., p. 4

136 Ibid.

137 Ibid., p. 5

138 'Threatened species list: vertebrate animals', Department of Primary Industries, Parks, Water and Environment, Tasmanian Government, updated 3 February 2021, dpipwe.tas.gov.au/conservation/threatened-species-and-communities/lists-of-threatened-species/threatened-species-vertebrates

139 Matthew Denholm, 'Tasmania's salmon trade casts deadly net', *Australian*, 22 June 2013, theaustralian.com.au/news/nation/tasmanias-salmon-trade-casts-deadly-net/news-story/af594bc90f2074dc9feob40378ec1039

140 Henry Zwartz, 'Dismay and despair as "dogs of the sea" threaten fishing livelihoods in Tasmania', ABC News, 29 August 2017, abc.net.au/news/2017-08-27/seals-in-north-west-tasmania-threatening-fishing-livelihood/8844066?nw=0. See also Craig Garland, Submission to the Legislative Council Fin Fish Farming in Tasmania Inquiry, 29 November 2019, parliament.tas.gov.au/ctee/Council/Submissions/FIN%20FISH/Submissions%201%20-%20125/77%20Craig%20Garland.pdf

141 Laura Beavis and April McLennan, 'DPIPWE gave salmon farm giant Tassal green light to trap seals', ABC News, 20 October 2020, abc.net.au/news/2020-10-20/dpipwe-consulted-tassal-about-media-questions-trapped-seals/12776358

142 Owen Evans, 'Salmon farmers using beanbag bullets to fend off seals in Australia', *Salmon Business*, 12 October 2018, salmonbusiness.com/salmon-farmers-using-beanbag-bullets-to-fend-off-seals-in-australia/

143 Henry Zwartz, 'Tasmania's salmon farms shooting thousands of non-lethal "beanbag" rounds at seals', ABC News, 12 October 2020,

abc.net.au/news/2018-10-12/seals-being-shot-with-thousands-of-beanbag-bullets-to-protect-s/10366006

144 Ken Hubbs and David Klinger, 'Impact Munitions Use: Types, Targets, Effects', Department of Justice, National Institute of Justice, February 2004, p. 3, ncjrs.gov/pdffiles1/nij/206089.pdf

Ryan Ho Kilpatrick, '"An eye for an eye": Hong Kong protests get figurehead in woman injured by police', *Guardian*, 16 August 2019, theguardian.com/world/2019/aug/16/an-eye-for-an-eye-hong-kong-protests-get-figurehead-in-woman-injured-by-police

Knvul Sheikh and David Montgomery, 'Rubber Bullets and Beanbag Rounds Can Cause Devastating Injuries', *New York Times*, 12 June 2020, nytimes.com/2020/06/12/health/protests-rubber-bullets-beanbag.html

145 Henry Zwartz, op cit., 'Tasmania's salmon farms shooting thousands of non-lethal "beanbag" rounds at seals'

146 Ibid.

147 Emily Baker, 'Hungry seals to cop water spray deterrent under new Tassal application', ABC News, 6 September 2020, abc.net.au/news/2019-09-06/salmon-farmers-seek-approval-to-use-water-streams-to-deter-seals/11482398

148 Ibid.

149 Aimee Kerr and Jason Scorse, 'The Use of Seal Bombs in California Fisheries', Center for the Blue Economy, 2018, p. 2, middlebury.edu/institute/sites/www.middlebury.edu.institute/files/2018-12/Seal%20Bombs%20in%20CA-%20Final.pdf

150 Ibid, p. 4

151 Henry Zwartz, op cit., 'Tasmania's salmon farms shooting thousands of non-lethal "beanbag" rounds at seals'

152 Anne E. Simonis et al., 'Seal Bomb Noise as a Potential Threat to Monterey Bay Harbor Porpoise', *Frontiers in Marine Science*, 13 March 2020, frontiersin.org/articles/10.3389/fmars.2020.00142/full#B79

153 'How do acoustic deterrent devices work?', Scottish Salmon Producers Organisation factsheet, undated, scottishsalmon.co.uk/facts/faqs/fish-health-welfare/how-do-acoustic-deterrent-devices-work

154 Memo to Marine Scotland, Scottish government from Head of Policy and Device, Scottish National Heritage, 28 July 2017, assets.

documentcloud.org/documents/6946928/SNH-Advice-to-MS-28
-07-2017-FOI.pdf

155 Anne E. Simonis et al., op cit.

156 Ibid.

157 Ibid.

158 Alistair Bland, 'California Fishermen Are Throwing Explosives at Sea Lions', *Hakai* magazine, coastal science and societies, 20 November 2017, hakaimagazine.com/news/california-fishermen-are-throwing-explosives-sea-lions/

159 Songhi Li et al., 'Potential impacts of shipping noise on Indo-Pacific humpback dolphins and implications for regulation and mitigation: a review', *Integrative Zoology*, 9 January 2018, onlinelibrary.wiley.com/doi/epdf/10.1111/1749-4877.12304

160 Rhianne Ward, Claire Charlton and Sacha Guggenheimer, 'Southern Right Whale (Eubalaena Australis) Acoustics at Fowlers Bay, South Australia', Internal report for Centre for Marine Science and Technology, Curtin University, July 2013, p. 11, cmst.curtin.edu.au/wp-content/uploads/sites/4/2017/06/CMST-Report-Fowlers-Bay-2013-RW-CC-SG.pdf

161 John Seeback, 'Action statement, Flora and Fauna Guarantee Act 1988, Department of Sustainability and Environment, Victorian government, 2004, p. 3, environment.vic.gov.au/__data/assets/pdf_file/0016/32371/Southern_Right_Whale_Eubalaena_australis.pdf

162 Hannah Blair et al., 'Evidence for ship noise impacts on humpback whale foraging behaviour', *Biology Letters*, Royal Society Publishing, August 2016, ncbi.nlm.nih.gov/pmc/articles/PMC5014013/

163 Chris Black, *White Pointer South*, Wellington Bridge Press, Hobart, 2010, p. 179

164 Case study, 'Growing the Tasmanian Atlantic salmon farming industry', CSIRO, Agriculture and Fisheries, updated 27 July 2020, csiro.au/en/About/Our-impact/Our-impact-in-action/Agriculture-and-Fisheries/Salmon

165 Ibid.

166 Michael Hortle, 'Salmon Farming in Tasmania', Australian Fisheries, November 1986, p. 19, nla.gov.au/nla.obj-740401462/view?sectionId=nla.obj-741799981&partId=nla.obj-740449552#page/n18/mode/1up

167 Huon Aquaculture Salmonid Industry Discussion Paper, 2018, p. 35, huonaqua.com.au/wp-content/uploads/2017/08/Huon-Aquaculture-Salmonid-Industry-Discussion-Paper.pdf

168 Waldo G. Nuez-Ortin et al., 'Liver proteome response of pre-harvest Atlantic salmon following exposure to elevated temperature', *BMC Genomics*, 12 February 2018, bmcgenomics.biomedcentral.com/articles/10.1186/s12864-018-4517-0

169 Mark Adams, 'Pathology of amoebic gill disease in Atlantic Salmon (Salmo salar L.)', PhD, University of Tasmania, 2003, p. 2, eprints.utas.edu.au/19177/1/whole_AdamsMark2003_thesis.pdf

170 Mark Adams et al., 'Sequential pathology after initial freshwater bath treatment for amoebic gill disease in cultured Atlantic salmon Salmo salar L', *Journal of Fish Diseases*, March 2004, researchgate.net/publication/5627312_Sequential_pathology_after_initial_freshwater_bath_treatment_for_amoebic_gill_disease_in_cultured_Atlantic_salmon_Salmo_salar_L

171 Claire M. Spillman and Alistair J. Hobday, 'Dynamical seasonal ocean forecasts to aid salmon farm management in a climate hotspot', *Climate Risk Management*, Elsevier B. V., 2013, p. 26, sciencedirect.com/science/article/pii/S2212096313000041#b0005

172 Amelia White, op cit., pp. 185–6

173 Ibid., p. 181

174 Tassal Sustainability Report 2020, p. 26, tassalgroup.com.au/our-planet/reports/sustainability/

175 Huon Aquaculture, Submission to the Legislative Council Fin Fish Farming in Tasmania Inquiry, November 2019, p. 47, parliament.tas.gov.au/ctee/council/Submissions/FIN%20FISH/Submissions%201%20-%20125/87%20Huon%20Aquaculture%20Company%20Pty%20Ltd.pdf

176 Eden Hynninen, 'Tasmania's green drought is no longer green', ABC News, 29 November 2019, abc.net.au/news/rural/2019-11-29/tasmanian-farmers-tackle-long-dry/11751280

177 Productivity Commission report, 'Australian Atlantic Salmon: Effects of Import Competition', 20 December 1996, p. 103, pc.gov.au/research/supporting/salmon/salmon.pdf

178 EPA Enquiries to Richard Flanagan, email, 30 October 2020

179 Melinda Huck, Submission to the Legislative Council Fin Fish Farming in Tasmania Inquiry, 29 November 2019, parliament.tas.gov.au/ctee/Council/Submissions/FIN%20FISH/Submissions%20126%20-%20223/210%20Melinda%20Huck_Redacted.pdf

180 Tony Mahood, Submission to the Legislative Council Fin Fish Farming in Tasmania Inquiry, 22 November 2019, parliament.tas.gov.au/ctee/Council/Submissions/FIN%20FISH/Submissions%201%20-%20125/25%20Tony%20Mahood.pdf

181 Dr Sharon Moore, Submission to the Legislative Council Fin Fish Farming in Tasmania Inquiry, date redacted, parliament.tas.gov.au/ctee/Council/Submissions/FIN%20FISH/Submissions%201%20-%20125/73%20Dr%20Sharon%20Moore_Redacted.pdf

182 US Department of Justice Command Center, memo for Dan Levin, Organization: Office of Legal, 30 December 2004, aclu.org/files/projects/foiasearch/ocr/DOJOLC001126.txt

183 Emilie Gramenz, 'Salmon farming giant Tassal to be probed over witness pulling out of aquaculture inquiry', ABC News, 9 February 2017, abc.net.au/news/2017-02-09/tassal-to-be-probed-over-influence-on-salmon-inquiry-witness/8255362

184 Monika Maedler, Tassal Company Secretary, to the Manager Listings, ASX Market Announcements, 24 October 2016, p. 5, asx.com.au/asxpdf/20161024/pdf/43c7b3pzv99j7x.pdf

185 Emilie Gramenz, op cit.

186 Harriet Aird, 'Tassal "should not be found in contempt" of aquaculture industry inquiry', ABC News, 9 August 2017, abc.net.au/news/2017-08-09/tassal-found-not-in-contempt-of-salmon-inquiry/8788106

187 Tassal, Environmental Impact Statement, Hamilton Recirculating Aquaculture System Hatchery, September 2019, epa.tas.gov.au/Documents/Tassal%20Operations%20Pty%20Ltd%20-%20Hamilton%20Recirculating%20Aquaculture%20System%20Hatchery,%20Ouse20-%20EIS.pdf

188 Tellingly, the distance of 850 metres is not given in any official documentation. It can only be obtained by using the non-scaled map of the site (showing the toxic effluent dam) in the EPA's final Environmental

Assessment Report, Recirculating Aquaculture System Hatchery, Ouse, November 2019, p. 9, in conjunction with the scaled map of the site (not showing the toxic effluent dam) in Tassal, Natural Values Asessment for Proposed Hatchery Facility as 56 Wooodmoor Road, Ouse, 30 July 2019, p. 8, note: left-hand dam to be used for toxic waste water. See epa.tas.gov.au/Documents/Tassal%20 Operations%20Pty%20Ltd%20-%20Hamilton%20Recirculating%20 Aquaculture%20System%20Hatchery,%20Ouse%20-%20EAR.pdf and epa.tas.gov.au/Documents/Tassal%20Operations%20Pty%20Ltd%20 -%20Hamilton%20Recirculating%20Aquaculture%20System%20 Hatchery,%20Ouse%20-%20Appendices.pdf

189 Nutes [sic] of the Special Planning Committee Meeting of the Central Highlands Council, 26 November 2019, (draft) (no final minutes publicly available), p. 31, centralhighlands.tas.gov.au/wp-content/ uploads/Draft-Special-Planning-Committee-Minutes.pdf

190 Annah Fromberg, 'Farmers fear runoff from proposed Tassal salmon hatchery', ABC News, 14 October 2019, abc.net.au/news/2019-10-14/ farmers-angry-over-proposed-salmon-farm/11599736

191 Jillian P. Fry et al., 'Environmental health impacts of feeding crops to farmed fish', *Environment International*, May 2016, sciencedirect.com/ science/article/pii/S0160412016300587#bb0160

192 Jean D. Brender, 'Prenatal Nitrate Intake from Drinking Water and Selected Birth Defects in Offspring of Participants in the National Birth Defects Prevention Study', *Environmental Health Perspectives*, September 2013, ncbi.nlm.nih.gov/pmc/articles/PMC3764078

193 L. Knobeloch et al., 'Blue babies and nitrate-contaminated well water', *Environmental Health Perspectives*, July 2000, ncbi.nlm.nih.gov/ pmc/articles/PMC1638204

194 Gabriel Gulis et al., 'An ecologic study of nitrate in municipal drinking water and cancer incidence in Trnava District, Slovakia', National Center for Biotechnology Information, March 2002, pubmed.ncbi. nlm.nih.gov/12051796/

195 Peter Headlam, Submission to the Legislative Council Fin Fish Farming in Tasmania Inquiry, 29 November 2019, parliament.tas.gov. au/ctee/council/Submissions/FIN%20FISH/Submissions%201%20-%20

125/54%20Peter%20Headlam_Redacted.pdf. See also Annah Fromberg, 'Farmers fear runoff from proposed Tassal salmon hatchery', op cit.

196 Caro Meldrum-Hanna, 'Huon Aquaculture takes Tasmanian Government to court over salmon farming in Macquarie Harbour', ABC News, 6 Feb. 2017; https://www.abc.net.au/news/2017-02-06/huon-aquaculture-lawsuit-tasmania-government-macquarie-harbour/8244330

197 Peter Headlam, op cit.

198 Adele Ferguson, 'Rio Tinto's executive cull shows "profit at all cost" cultures no longer cut it', *Sydney Morning Herald*, 12 September 2020, smh.com.au/business/banking-and-finance/rio-tinto-s-executive-cull-shows-profit-at-all-cost-cultures-no-longer-cut-it-20200911-p55utf.html

199 'Aquaculture Stocks on the ASX: An In-Depth Guide', Capitalisticman.com, 13 April 2019, capitalisticman.com/aquaculture-companies-on-the-asx-an-in-depth-guide/

200 Kenneth M. Hayne, 'Royal Commission into Misconduct in the Banking, Superannuation and Financial Services Industry', Commonwealth of Australia, 2019, p. 37, financialservices.royalcommission.gov.au/Pages/reports.html#final

201 Adele Ferguson, op cit.

202 Brynn O'Brien, 'David Murray lacks 2020 board vision', *Australian Financial Review*, 27 August 2020, afr.com/policy/economy/david-murray-lacks-2020-board-vision-20200826-p55pc9

203 Matt Smith, 'Warning on fish-farm death traps', *Mercury*, 13 August 2016, themercury.com.au/news/tasmania/warning-on-fishfarm-death-traps/news-story/4758d2b45248215cdb4fcaf1bf1a7fa6

204 Anna Fromberg, 'Giant salmon ships bound for Tasmania, as local sailors told to "be on the lookout"', ABC News, 19 October 2019, abc.net.au/news/2019-10-19/river-derwent-sailors-concern-over-new-salmon-wellboats/11617610

205 'Mornings with Leon Compton', '"Someone will be seriously hurt or even killed": MAST boss warns about dangers of marine debris', ABC Radio, 27 February 2020, abc.net.au/radio/hobart/programs/mornings/mast-boss-warns-about-dangers-of-marine-debris/12006424

206 'Mornings with Leon Compton', ABC Radio, 11 August 2020

207 Lucy Adams, 'Is there a problem with salmon farming?', BBC News, 20 May 2019, bbc.com/news/uk-scotland-48266480

208 Leanne Minshull, Bill Browne, 'Making mountains out of minnows. Salmon in the Tasmania economy', Australia Institute, July 2019, p. 2, australiainstitute.org.au/wp-content/uploads/2020/12/P733-Mountains -out-of-minnows-Web_1.pdf

209 Lucy Adams, op cit.

210 Michael Hortle, op cit., p. 19, Productivity Commission Report, op cit., p. viii

211 Mark Kurlansky, 'Net loss: the high price of salmon farming', *Guardian*, 15 September 2020, theguardian.com/news/2020/sep/15/ net-loss-the-high-price-of-salmon-farming

212 Salmon farms are meant to have no visible impact beyond 35 metres of their lease. This Neighbours of Fish Farming footage shows a dying reef at Huon Island some kilometres from the nearest salmon farm: youtube.com/watch?v=wQ95F9MQMPQ&feature=youtu.be

213 Kasey Wilkins, 'The Bruny Island residents telling Tassal to abandon D'Entrecasteaux Channel', *Mercury*, 11 October 2020, themercury. com.au/news/tasmania/the-bruny-island-residents-telling-tassal -to-abandon-the-dentrecasteaux-channel/news-story/4c2a024ffff64ae b53a36f475479e40e

214 Peter Boyer, 'When experts speak on salmon industry, we deserve more than spin', *Mercury*, 3 November 2020, themercury.com.au/ news/opinion/talking-point-when-experts-speak-we-deserve-more- than-selfserving-spin-in-response/news-story/30f0405b6ecf17a0a f85bb2a4e953697

215 Ibid., p. 103

216 Productivity Commission, 'Australian Atlantic Salmon', 1996, p. xiv, pc.gov.au/research/supporting/salmon/salmon.pdf

217 Ibid., p. 28

218 Ibid.

219 'Rundle's Directions Statement a year on', *Examiner*, 13 April 1998, examiner.com.au/story/640435/rundles-directions-statement-a -year-on/

220 Chris Well, Submission to the Legislative Council Fin Fish Farming in Tasmania Inquiry, 1 November 2019, parliament.tas.gov.au/ctee/ Council/Submissions/FIN%20FISH/Submissions%201%20-%20 125/6%20Chris%20Wells_Redacted.pdf

221 David Killick, 'Concerns over seal welfare near Tassal pens', *Mercury*, 21 October 2020

222 Editorial, *Mercury*, 2 November 2016

223 Tassal, Submission to the Legislative Council Fin Fish Farming in Tasmania Inquiry, 29 November 2019, p. 7, parliament.tas.gov.au/ ctee/Council/Submissions/FIN%20FISH/Submissions%201%20-%20 125/83%20Tassal%20Group.pdf

224 Leanne Minshull, Bill Browne, Australia Institute, op cit., p. 1

225 Federal Group employment figure, treasury.tas.gov.au/Documents/ 6.%20Federal%20Group.PDF
Tourism employment figure, tourismtasmania.com.au/industry/facts
Salmon industry figure, tai.org.au/sites/default/files/P733%20 Mountains%20out%20of%20minnows%20%5BWeb%5D_1.pdf
Claim salmon 'major industry', DPIPWE (Tasmania) Marine Farming Branch, 'Marine Farming – Aquaculture,' (website) 10 November 2020, dpipwe.tas.gov.au/sea-fishing-aquaculture/marine-farming-aquaculture

226 Productivity Commission, 'Australian Atlantic Salmon', pc.gov.au/ research/supporting/salmon/salmon.pdf

227 Department of Agriculture, Water and the Environment, 'Australian fisheries and aquaculture outlook 2020: Salmonids', agriculture.gov. au/abares/research-topics/fisheries/fisheries-economics/fisheries- forecasts#salmonids
Department of Primary Industries, Parks, Water and Environment, 'Sustainable industry growth plan for the salmon industry', p. 6, dpipwe.tas.gov.au/Documents/salmonplan.pdf

228 Jason Holland, 'Scottish salmon production increased 30 percent in 2019', *Seafood Source*, 19 October 2020, seafoodsource.com/news/ aquaculture/scottish-salmon-production-increased-30-percent

229 Geoffrey Swan, 'Who's in Charge of the Huon Valley Council?', *Tasmanian Times*, 25 May 2020, tasmaniantimes.com/2020/05/whos-in -charge-of-the-huon-valley-council/

230 'Dead Loss. The high cost of poor farming practices and mortalities on salmon farms', *Just Economics*, February 2021, justeconomics.co.uk/health-and-well-being/dead-loss

231 Oliver Morrison, 'Salmon farming urged to boost tech investment in face of "significant environmental threats"' *Food Navigator*, 9 June 2020, foodnavigator.com/Article/2020/06/09/Salmon-farming-urged-to-boost-tech-investment-in-face-of-significant-environmental-threats

232 Brad Thompson, 'Takeover suitors circle salmon farmer Huon', *Australian Financial Review*, 26 February 2021, afr.com/companies/agriculture/takeover-suitors-circle-salmon-farmer-huon-20210226-p576a8

233 Tim Boreham, 'What are the ASX stocks vulnerable to a short squeeze?', Smallcaps.com, 11 February 2021, smallcaps.com.au/what-asx-stocks-vulnerable-to-a-short-squeeze/

234 Michelle Pears, Submission to the Legislative Council Fin Fish Farming in Tasmania Inquiry, 26 November 2019, parliament.tas.gov.au/ctee/Council/Submissions/FIN%20FISH/Submissions%201%20-%20125/32%20Michelle%20Pears_Redacted.pdf

235 Christos Lees, Submission to the Legislative Council Fin Fish Farming in Tasmania Inquiry, 29 November 2019, parliament.tas.gov.au/ctee/Council/Submissions/FIN%20FISH/Submissions%201%20-%20125/62%20Christo%20Lees.pdf

236 Denis Mermet, Submission to the Legislative Council Fin Fish Farming in Tasmania Inquiry, 26 November 2019, parliament.tas.gov.au/ctee/Council/Submissions/FIN%20FISH/Submissions%201%20-%20125/9%20Denis%20Mermet_Redacted.pdf

237 Mabs Mollineaux, Submission to the Legislative Council Fin Fish Farming in Tasmania Inquiry, 29 November 2019, parliament.tas.gov.au/ctee/Council/Submissions/FIN%20FISH/Submissions%201%20-%20125/86%20Mabs%20Mollineaux.pdf

238 Alan Kemp and Lisa Litjens, Submission to the Legislative Council Fin Fish in Tasmania Inquiry, November 2019, p. 27, parliament.tas.gov.au/ctee/Council/Submissions/FIN%20FISH/Submissions%201%20-%20125/41%20Neighbours%20of%20Fish%20Farming.pdf

239 Lynda House, Submission to the Legislative Council Fin Fish Farming in Tasmania Inquiry, 22 November 2019, parliament.tas.gov.au/ ctee/Council/Submissions/FIN%20FISH/Submissions%201%20-%20 125/24%20Lynda%20House.pdf

240 Chris Wells, Submission to the Legislative Council Fin Fish Farming in Tasmania Inquiry, 1 November 2019, parliament.tas.gov.au/ctee/ Council/Submissions/FIN%20FISH/Submissions%201%20-%20125/6 %20Chris%20Wells_Redacted.pdf

241 Tony Mahood, Submission to the Legislative Council Fin Fish Farming in Tasmania Inquiry, op cit.

242 Susan Westcott, Submission to the Legislative Council Fin Fish in Tasmania Inquiry, 14 November 2019, parliament.tas.gov.au/ctee/ Council/Submissions/FIN%20FISH/Submissions%201%20-%20 125/14%20Susan%20Westcott_Redacted.pdf

243 Simon Allston, Janeil Hall, Submission to the Legislative Council Fin Fish Farming in Tasmania Inquiry, November 2019, parliament. tas.gov.au/ctee/Council/Submissions/FIN%20FISH/Submissions%20 1%20-%20125/43a%20Simon%20Allston%20&%20Dr%20Janeil%20 Hall%20Signed_Redacted.pdf

244 Matt Maloney, 'Tasmanian government says arson penalties are toughest in country', *Examiner*, 2 January 2020, examiner.com.au/ story/6564102/government-defends-laws-around-arson/?cs=12

245 Leon Compton, 'Huon Aquaculture lease move approval angers fishers, conservationists', ABC News, 17 August 2018, abc.net.au/ news/2018-08-17/huon-aquaculture-lease-move-anger/10133452

246 Derwent Estuary Program Ltd, Submission on Storm Bay Marine Farming Development Plans/Environmental Impact Statements, 17 January 2018, derwentestuary.org.au/assets/DEP_Storm_Bay_ submission.pdf

247 Lydia Mulvaney and Josh Petri, 'The Beyond Meat of Fish Is Coming', Bloomberg, 12 June 2019, bloomberg.com/news/articles/2019-06-12/ there-s-already-a-race-to-become-the-beyond-meat-of-fish

248 Aslen Wilder, 'Legendary Vish Rebrands . . .', The Spoon, 12 February 2021, thespoon.tech/legendary-vish-rebrands-to-revo-foods-plans-to- host-tasting-for-3d-printed-salmon-soon/

Flora Southey, '3D Printed Fish: Plant-based salmon with "complex structure" under development for EU market', *Foodnavigator*, 6 July 2020, foodnavigator.com/Article/2020/07/06/3D-printed-fish-Plant-based-salmon-with-complex-structure-under-development-for-EU-market

249 Norwegian experts expect land-based systems to halve their electricity usage per kilogram of salmon produced, see Ulf Winthern et al., 'Greenhouse gas emissions of Norwegian seafood products in 2017', Trondheim, 2020, p. 83, sintef.no/contentassets/25338e561f1a4 270a59ce25bcbc926a2/report-carbon-footprint-norwegian-seafood-products-2017_final_040620.pdf/

250 Cliff White, 'Atlantic Sapphire building USD 350 million land-based salmon farm in Miami', *Seafood Source*, 19 March 2017, seafoodsource.com/news/aquaculture/atlantic-sapphire-building-usd-350-million-land-based-salmon-farm-in-miami

251 Ibid.

252 Sarah Cox, 'The Rise of the Land Salmon', *The Narwhal*, 19 December 2019, thenarwhal.ca/rise-of-land-salmon-farming

253 Dan Gibson, '5000t capacity just the beginning for $80 million Saudi RAS farm', *Undercurrent News*, 26 August 2019, undercurrentnews.com/2019/08/26/5000t-capacity-just-the-beginning-for-80m-saudi-salmon-ras-farm/; Sarah Cox, op cit.

254 Owen Evans, 'Dongwon Industries say they will produce 20,000 tonnes at South Korean land-based salmon farm', *Salmon Business*, 1 September 2019, salmonbusiness.com/dongwon-industries-say-they-will-produce-20000-tonnes-at-south-korean-land-based-salmon-farm/

255 'Is RAS ready to shine?', *World Fishing and Aquaculture,* 2 January 2020, worldfishing.net/news101/Comment/analysis/is-ras-ready-to-shine

256 Editorial staff, '66,000 tonnes land-based salmon farm project announced', *Salmon Business*, 29 October 2020, salmonbusiness.com/66000-tonnes-land-based-salmon-farm-project-announced/

257 'Siemens signs letter of intent with Swedish RAS megafarm', *Undercurrent News*, 25 June 2020, undercurrentnews.com/2020/06/25/siemens-signs-letter-of-intent-with-swedish-ras-megafarm

'Giant Swedish RAS project picks China's iCell to handle water cleaning', *Undercurrent News*, 13 October 2020, undercurrentnews.

com/2020/10/13/giant-swedish-ras-project-picks-chinas-icell-to-handle
-water-cleaning/

258 Aslak Berge, 'Inside this disused mine, a 100,000 tonne salmon farm is
being planned, one of the world's largest', *Salmon Business*, 8 February
2021, salmonbusiness.com/inside-this-disused-mine-a-100000-tonne
-salmon-farm-is-being-planned-one-of-the-worlds-largest/

259 'To convert 120,000 tonnes of sludge annually into energy and saleable
proteins from farming in a closed mine', iLaks.no, 2 February 2021,
ilaks.no/skal-omdanne-120-000-tonn-slam-arlig-til-energi-og-
salgbare-proteiner-fra-oppdrett-i-nedlagt-gruve/

260 'Swedish RAS park signs letter of intent with state-owned green
energy supplier', *Undercurrent News*, 16 July 2020, undercurrentnews.
com/2020/07/16/swedish-ras-park-signs-letter-of-intent-with-state-
owned-green-energy-supplier/

261 Ulf Winthern et al., 'Greenhouse gas emissions' op cit., p. 68

262 Sandra Eady et al., 'Carbon footprint for Australian agricultural
products and downstream food products in the supermarket',
Australian Life Cycle Assessment Society 7th Conference, Melbourne,
9–10 March 2011, refereed conference paper, abstract, publications.
csiro.au/rpr/pub?pid=csiro:EP104701

263 Frances Vinall, 'Salmon to hit the skies', *Examiner*, 24 April 2020,
examiner.com.au/story/6734661/salmon-to-hit-the-skies-via-new-
freight-planes-for-overseas-exports/

264 Beyhan de Jong, 'Aquaculture 2.0: RAS Is Driving Change – Land-
Based Farming Is Set to Disrupt Salmon', RaboResearch, Rabobank,
October 2019, research.rabobank.com/far/en/sectors/animal-protein/
Aquaculture-2point0-RAS.html#
See also Jason Holland, 'RAS to disrupt the salmon sector . . .' *Seafood
Source*, 18 October 2019, seafoodsource.com/news/aquaculture/
ras-to-disrupt-the-salmon-sector-within-the-next-decade-says-
rabobank; Owen Evans, 'Rabobank's best case RAS production
scenario is €3.5 per kilo in 10 years', *Salmon Business*, October 2018,
salmonbusiness.com/rabobanks-best-case-ras-production-scenario
-is-e3-5-per-kilo-in-10-years/

265 Owen Evans, op cit.

266 Jane Byrne, 'Rabobank's view . . .', *Feed Navigator*, 27 November 2020, feednavigator.com/Article/2020/11/27/Rabobank-s-view-Very-tight-salmon-supply-expected-in-2021-all-eyes-on-RAS-developments -bullish-forecast-for-shrimp-prices-and-higher-demand-seen-for-fishmeal

267 Huon Aquaculture, Submission to the Legislative Council Fin Fish Farming in Tasmania Inquiry, November 2019, p. 29, parliament.tas. gov.au/ctee/council/Submissions/FIN%20FISH/Submissions%201%20 -%20125/87%20Huon%20Aquaculture%20Company%20Pty%20Ltd. pdf

268 Tassal, 'Environmental Impact Statement Hamilton Recirculating Aquaculture System Hatchery', September 2018, p. 105, epa.tas. gov.au/Documents/Tassal%20Operations%20Pty%20Ltd%20-%20 Hamilton%20Recirculating%20Aquaculture%20System%20Hatchery, %20Ouse%20-%20EIS.pdf

269 Huon Aquaculture, Submission to Legislative Council Fin Fish Farming in Tasmania Inquiry, op cit., p. 29

270 Tom Seaman, 'Marubeni, Nissui, snap up Danish RAS salmon farmer to kickstart move into sector', *Undercurrent News*, 16 April 2020 undercurrentnews.com/2020/04/16/marubeni-nissui-snap-up-danish -ras-salmon-farmer-to-kickstart-move-into-sector/

RICHARD FLANAGAN'S novels have received numerous honours and are published in forty-two countries. He won the Booker Prize for *The Narrow Road to the Deep North* and the Commonwealth Prize for *Gould's Book of Fish*. A rapid on the Franklin River is named after him.